Broken Narritives

For we are God's masterpiece. He has created us anew in Christ Jesus, so we can do the good things he planned for us long ago.

~Ephesians 2:10, NLT

Broken Narratives

Restoration in the Broken Pieces of Our Lives

Lucrecia Slater

LSSlater Publishing
P.O. Box 20276
Clarksville, TN 37042
www.lsslater.com

Cover Design: Nydia Pastoriza with sazzyreaders.com
Interior Design: Nydia Pastoriza with sazzyreaders.com
Publisher: LSSlater Publishing
Editor: Kiva Harper As the editor if she/he wants their name on the inside of the book.
ISBN: 9780578198095
First Edition

I grew into a woman who was broken and had very little hope. I wanted to believe that God could use me, but the chaos of my life distorted the thoughts. It was through the life of a woman in scripture, where God would teach me not only was everything I went through necessary, but it all had purpose.

Contents

To my daughters, Kimarra and Satroyia...

With God's ability, you two help make me to be the woman I hope you will one day be proud to call your mother. I love you with every fiber of my being. Love you to the moon and beyond, mom/mommy.

Prologue

I wondered what she was like. I wondered how she viewed herself. I mean really viewed herself. You know those inward conversations, images, and observations we entertain within ourselves? Yeah, that's what I'm talking about, the real view of herself. I wondered how she came to the point where she accepted the validation of the broken narrative of her life. What happened to her where she concluded that this is what the sum of her life was? She walked alone. No girlfriends to chat about how their day went. No children to shoo away from the pantry. Not even family to be an anchor for some of the turbulence in her life. But she wasn't alone in companionship. She had that. And a lot of it. See, this woman was a lot like many of us are today.

We get injured in areas of our lives and eventually become cripple. In our afflictions, instead of seeking the right help and counsel, we turn to a "drug" of choice. Whether that be a string of relationships, sexual encounters, food, shopping, or whatever the vice- we enable our disability. We eventually validate those broken areas of our lives, allowing them to become our truth. That's what this woman did. She settled in the comforts of dysfunction and chose to rest in this repetitious cycle of her life. She had been in a string of broken relationships. And the one she was in now wasn't legitimately her own. So, who is this woman you may ask? Well I'm glad you did! She's the Samaritan woman at the well.

In John 4, we are introduced to the woman. The scene is descriptive so we get a good visual of what's going on. Jesus and His disciples arrived at Jacob's well. Tired from the day's teachings and journey, Jesus went and rested by the well while His disciples went into the village for food (John 4:8). As He waited by the well, which was a strategic move, the Samaritan woman entered.

I must pause right here because this is one of the many ways of God that gets me. You see, He doesn't wait until we half way have it together to enter our lives. He doesn't wait until we are walking that straight and narrow path. The truth and fact is, we will NEVER have it together and we will always get off the path. In Luke chapter 5, Jesus made the deliberate decision to step right into the middle of Peter's frustrations when Jesus chose to get into Peter's boat and continue His sermon. This happened right after a disappointing night (all night I might add) of Peter not catching one fish. It is right smack dab in the middle of our mess where two things happen: we realize God's glory and so does everyone else around us. Peter's life after Jesus' entrance into that boat was never the same, and so was the case with the Samaritan woman.

Jesus chose that day, that spot, that town, that well, and in that hour to meet up with the woman. She was neck deep in her mess and Jesus was there to reveal God's glory and forever change her life. The mere fact that Jesus interacted with a Samaritan, and a woman at that, would have been enough to have caused an uproar. But thanks be to God, there are no gender biases with Him.

So here we are at the juicy part of the woman's story. Jesus asks the woman for water. I can imagine how this would play out in modern times. Can you? Some random man standing next to a well sees us struggling with this huge bucket and has the audacity to ask for some water! Not only do we give dagger eyes, but we fix our lips to tell him off right where he stands. "How dare you ask me to get you some water! You see me struggling with this...you should be asking to help ME get some water!" Of course, we'd have the variety of flailing arms and body gestures to go along with it. Can you catch that visual? I chuckle to myself as I digress.

So as Jesus asked the woman for a drink, instead of tongue lashing him, she was actually surprised. Surprised by the fact that a Jew was speaking to a Samaritan woman! Her response to Him was, "You are a Jew, and I am a Samaritan woman. Why are You asking me for a drink?" (John 4:9, NLT). Just what Jesus needed, a door in which to enter. And it came in her response to Him.

As we read on throughout this conversation, we see that the woman was being drawn to Jesus. She dismissed the idea of the two cultural boundaries between the two. She wanted to know more of what He had to say. She was intrigued by this "water" He kept speaking of. After some time, Jesus made His move. "'Go and get your husband,' Jesus told her' (John 4:16). Her response was the reason why Jesus had strategically chosen that spot to stop. Her response revealed the broken narrative that she had come to adopt as the normalcy of her life. And He was there to fix that! But not only would her life be transformed, but literally a generation of people after her.

"I don't have a husband," the woman replied. Jesus said, "You're right!

9

You don't have a husband---for you have had five husbands, and you aren't even married to the man you're living with now. You certainly spoke the truth!"' (John 4:17-18, NLT). She was locked in. After revealing the mess under the covers, she declared Jesus to be a prophet. But then she did something that many of us do, she quickly diverted the conversation. Instead of the Samaritan woman homing in on Jesus' divine knowledge, she changed the subject completely. Now I don't know if this was an intentional move, the text doesn't specify that, but she made it. Sound familiar? I know it does to me. Even when the sheets have been pulled back and the nasty underneath is revealed, in attempts to save some sort of face or ego, we justify, make excuses, or deny altogether. Because to stand and face the reflection looking back at us, we must be willing to allow others in on it as well. We must allow vulnerability and humility to enter in and begin the work. The truth of authenticity takes over where pride and embarrassment leaves off.

This book is not a self-help type of book, though I believe you will gain much insight into your own life. Neither is this book is a tell-all, expose all type of book. Rather, this book tells of a woman who was broken almost her entire life. How she has overcome many hurdles, but has many more in front of her to successfully clear. As you read, you will discover that her life was riddled with false validations; some that were imposed on her from birth and others that were self-inflicted.

This woman is me.

I want to invite you in. I want you to understand that we ALL have fallen short of God's glory. I want you to see through my life that you still have a chance at opening the door to authenticity and transparency and allowing God to do the work, to heal you, so you won't pass on the legacy of a broken life to your daughters. Most of all, you will receive hope. Hope to know that even amid your own broken life, God has a plan and a purpose for that brokenness.

Broken Narratives is my story, yet a story I believe many of us can relate to. We've lived in the realm of brokenness until it's become many of our norms. It would feel out of our element once we start to receive healing and restoration. Understand that the broken pieces of your life and my life were never meant to be in vain. They were never meant to be overlooked and thrown by the wayside. God has always had very good uses and plans for those pieces. He has put His stamp of approval on every piece and qualified them to do the work that needs to be done in another woman's life.

As we take this journey together, you will learn how God is molding you and I into His original blueprint as well as using those broken narratives for His benefit and glory. In our brokenness lies one of the most beautiful love stories ever told...the shining Knight after His love, you and me.

So, please, find your favorite quiet place to sit, with a comfy blanket, with your favorite drink (coffee, latte, hot chocolate) and maybe a box of Kleenex and let's go on this journey together, shall we?

1

Protect the Innocence

"I should have lost my life at the age of 3."
---Lucrecia Slater

My little legs could barely keep up. It was just as sticky and hot inside the old house as it was outside. It was a very hot summer day in Florida. In the silent swiftness of my mother, she grabbed my arm and we bolted out of the tattered screen door. Her light yellow dress flapped behind her like a cape as we ran. I kept trying to look back to get a glimpse at what we were running from. My mother, holding her swollen belly, cleared the raggedy stairs while still tightly clutching my arm.

As we rounded the corner of the house that's when I heard the door behind us bust open. He had something in his hand that made loud, popping noises. My mom positioned me behind her leg as we hid behind a corner of the house. My little mind was confused from the commotion, but understood enough to know it wasn't good.

The man was in fast pursuit of us and my mom took off again, still holding her belly with the baby inside We ran around the back and to the other side of the house. I don't know how I realized it, but the thing in the man's hand making loud, popping noises was actually a gun. And with every few steps he shot at us. "Why is he shooting at us, ma?" I asked as I was half running, half being drug by my mother. "He trying to kill us," were the only words she got out. He ended up emptying his gun trying to kill us. The man was my unborn sister's father. Thirty-three years later, I realized at the age of three, I had become a character in my mother's broken narrative.

Many times, things show up in our lives. They show up with a blaring "I'm here!!" In a whirlwind, we're trying to figure out life, figure our problems out, figure out the chaos and everything else.

I don't profess, by a long shot, to be a psychologist nor any professional like that, but what I have noticed, in my own life and the lives of others, is that when red flags show up, instead of stopping everything to figure out the origin of those flags, we usually just accept them, like the lady at the well eventually did.

For example, at 3 years old, a young child is at the age where he or she can somewhat understand a situation, at least generally speaking. Factually speaking, at this age, children are explorers. They are learning their surroundings and the "why's" of those surroundings. They are some of the most curious and fearless creatures I've ever seen and if any of you reading this have children or have been around children, then you can definitely attest to this. Riddling us with thousands of questions relentlessly, jumping off the top step when they've clearly been warned of impeding danger... I digress.

At this age, they are becoming. They are becoming little products of their environment. Now, I know we've heard statements like "You/We/I are not/am not products of our environment." I used to say that. The truth is, we are. We learn how to talk, act, do, and be by our surrounding environment. Inadvertently, we become what we are exposed to. Of course, this doesn't apply in all situations. Let's just say in mine it did.

When I think back to when I was 3, an image of my youngest daughter comes up. As a matter of fact, the image and thought hit me like a sack of metal bricks. It was that somber moment that I realized the importance of the role I have in my children's lives.

My 4-year-old is a mess, I tell you! She's independent, smart, funny, and a bit bossy and she knows it. Her eyes glow when something intriguing catches her attention on the television. She is feisty, quick to defend herself from her older sister, who always taunts her (I guess that's how older siblings get their entertainment, I did the same thing). She loves reading or being read to. She is eager to learn and discover. My daughter really intrigues me. To see her emerge into life with pure innocence puts so much pressure on me. I mean, I am in charge of this little life. In charge of the direction it takes, at least while she's under my roof and care.

I didn't even have this reality check with my oldest daughter. And decades later, it hit me of how important it is for parents to be the safeguards to their children. Granted, we won't be able to protect them from everything and it's necessary for them to go through some things on their own, but to place a child amid a shattered life and hand them the baton like "here ya go, it's your turn to fight," isn't fair...it's not fair at all. I wonder if any of this at all was the case for the Samaritan woman. What forged her path to the destination in which she found herself?

I'm sure my mother had no idea what she had injected into our lives. She raised us the best way she knew how with the best resources available, or at least I choose to think that. However, in the unspoken, unseen realm, chains are passed on through the generations. What our great, great, great grandmother struggled with, here we are in modern times still fighting. The contender may look different but the fight is still the same.

#coffeemoments
The contender may look different but the fight is still the same

I watched my mother fight. She fought for her very existence. Her fighting led to many retreats, many wounds, many setbacks. We moved a lot. In and around the city we lived in, we moved. I went to three elementary schools. Just as I got comfortable, the fight of my mother's life began again and it was time to uproot. Moving and uprooting became our normal. When in fact, that was the complete opposite.

When we enter the doors of parenthood, mindsets and habits should shift. From the point of the birth of a child, it's no longer about us. Everything we thought mattered becomes irrelevant. One of the greatest things that matters is the wellbeing of that child. We take on an unspoken oath to do everything within our power to protect our children and raise them with the direction and guidance of the Lord (Proverbs 22:6).

There was nothing written in the Bible to speculate about the Samaritan woman's mother. We are only left with what we know about the woman. I want to bring our attention to this point---the woman ended up alone. She had been out casted by her own people. What doors were opened in her own childhood that could have led her to this point in her adulthood? What if, in the mess of our own lives, we expose our children to situations that wind up having lasting, negative effects in their lives? What if, in

14

the mess of our own lives, we plant unhealthy seeds into the soil of our children's lives? What happens when the things that never got dealt with in our lives start to reflect in our children's lives? These are a few of the many questions I ponder over the Samaritan woman's life, in my own life growing up, and even my own behavior in my children's lives. And I also want you to ponder over these questions.

We are our children's first everything. First impression. First example. First leader. You get my drift. Aside from some unfortunate circumstances and the manner in which children enter into the world, many of us intentionally make the decision to become parents. We make the conscious decision that we will be responsible for the little ones, until they grow and enter adulthood. However, because many of us aren't aware of our own brokenness, we really don't know what we set our children up for.

2

Exposed: The Beginning

"But their evil intentions will be exposed when the light shines
on them, for the light makes everything visible..."
---Ephesians 5:13-14 (NLT)

See for the woman at the well, the way she lived could have very well manifested from a seed planted within her from her upbringing. Now, this is all speculation since we have nothing to go off of prior to her encounter with Jesus. Her habits, her patterns, her thought processes, her way of life was her norm. She had gotten used to the fact that she would walk life out alone and would receive odd stares from others. It's odd how in her desolate valley full of bones, is where Jesus chose to meet her and pick up, restore, and use those bones.

My baby girl loves running around the house with no bottoms on. Whether it's a skirt, dress, shorts, or pants, the minute she hits the door from a trip or running errands, she's ready to exit out of them. She's even asked me in an aisle at Wal-Mart, "Mommy, can I take my pants off now?" with the most serious of expressions. I always said, "Baby cakes, you don't want everybody seeing your "petunia". Just wait until we get home." And believe me, she holds me to it.

At the last kick of the restricting garment, she takes off sprinting through the house, just as liberated as she can be. It doesn't stop there. Before and after her bath, my daughter manages to find a way to escape my grip and run all through the house, "butt-booty" naked. I can hear her laugh as she meets up with a family member and shakes her little bottom.

I can hear comments from my oldest daughter, "Uh-uh Troi, you need to get back in the room now!" or my husband, "Girl what you are doing running through the house naked?" She's unbothered. She continues frolicking until I finally chase her down. When I catch her and hold her in my arms, there's always a joyful twinkle in her eyes, one that's filled with glee, excitement, and pleasure.

My daughter is almost completely unaware of her exposure. Her trust of care and protection is automatic in her surroundings. She's oblivious to the innocence and purity she possesses or the threat that lies ahead in the future if she's not aware of it.

I find myself daydreaming a lot when I look at my daughter as she dances around in her birthday suit. I'm taken back to my own childhood where I was exposed to things no child at that age should be exposed to. I saw things that I carry to this day.

We've all heard the phrase, "the eyes are the windows to the soul." I'm not sure where that saying originated from, but I believe the idea was taken from the scripture, Matthew 6:22-23 (NIV) which says *"The eye is the lamp of the body. So, if your eye is healthy, your whole body will be full of light, but if your eye is bad, your whole body will be full of darkness."* From the minute we set our eyes on something, it enters our brains. And from the brain it makes an imprint in our minds. So even though we may forget something later down the road, that memory is still there.

I remember my first visual encounter with anything sexual. I was five years old. My mom and I were riding with a group of her friends one evening. I sat in the back in between two young men. Out of nowhere, the guy to my right unzipped his pants and exposed himself. I had no clue what I was looking at and why he was exposing himself. I remained quiet as I watched the man please himself. My mom was in the front seat totally oblivious to what was taking place right behind her. After he finished with his business, he slipped himself back into his pants, readjusted himself and grabbed me. He placed me on his lap and tried talking to me. I could feel his still fully erect manhood on my tiny backside but again, I had no idea what was taking place. I suppose it was God that prevented things from going further because we had arrived at our destination.

The next incident took place while I was in the 1st grade. I sat not far from this other little girl. She and I weren't really friends, but we played together every now and then. During one particular day at quiet time, I watched as she put her hand in her pants. Curious, I continued watching. After putting her hand in her pants, she started moving up and down. After some time, she noticed me looking at her and gave me a frown and stuck her tongue out at me. The girl did this day after day. It wasn't long before I started mirroring her behavior.

I didn't have the slightest clue what the point was, I just knew my hand was in my pants on my private parts and it felt weird. But I did it because that's what I saw. And what I saw started to stick in my mind and boy did it imprint. I'm not sure whatever happened to that girl or what even triggered her to start doing that and I won't speculate. But as for me, it opened many doors.

I never told my mom or anybody what I was doing. I didn't think of it as anything important or wrong. But that wasn't the only problem I dealt with. I also saw the struggle my mother had with her relationship with my father.

I'm still gripped with emotion even now as I talk about my father. This is one of many memories that holds the answer to where many roots stemmed from. Going back to when I was 3-years-old from being shot at by my sister's father, it was also during this time when I heard my father deny me in court in front of a judge. I stood silently next to my mom as she let my father have an earful of her thoughts (not good ones I might add). The judge said looked directly at my father and said, "Sir, if this lil' girl didn't look like you spat her out of your mouth then maybe I would consider that she wasn't yours." That still didn't stop my father from trying to deny me.

I didn't understand it then, but he had planted the seeds of abandonment and rejection into my innocent spirit. As I grew older, I saw him come around from time to time. He lived about a fifteen-minute walk away from my house, but I saw him sparingly. It was as if he lived in another city or state.

He came around, bounced me on his shoulders for a bit, he and my mother had conversations and then he left. He spent a great deal of time in and out of jail, mainly because he constantly tried avoiding paying my mom child support. His visits became more distant. Eventually, he stopped coming around altogether. The next time I saw my father I was around 7 years old, an already messed up little girl. I guess he decided to want to try to make the relationship work with my mom, but boy was that a big mistake.

We lived in a duplex at the time. Those walls were ridiculously thin. The construction was poorly done as the roaches from our neighbors' apartment took it upon themselves to mosey over through the cracks in the wall into our apartment and make themselves at home.

My dad came over. I don't remember much of what transpired while they sat and talked in the front room but I remember he reeked of alcohol and he kept raising his voice at my mom. I went into the room I shared with my middle sister. She started crying as I did my best to console her.

As soon as I stepped into my room, my dad grabbed my mother by the throat and started choking her. Through gasps of air, my mother yelled for me to go and grab a knife. I instantly burst out into tears and did as she said. The first knife I found was a sharp, brown handled knife. I was familiar with it because I burned the handle of it on top of the stove when I learned how to make my own grill cheese sandwich. I grabbed it and ran back to my mom, who was desperately trying to fight my dad's hands off her throat. Through another loud, gaspy breath, my mother told me to stab him. Again, sobbing loudly, I did what she said. I started stabbing him in the left bicep like it was a piece of meat. I kept yelling, "Get your hands off my momma! Get your hands off my momma!" as I kept stabbing him.

After a while, I started seeing blood. But that didn't stop me. I was going to keep stabbing him as long as he kept hurting my mom. He finally let her go and pushed me aside and left. I dropped the knife and grabbed my mom who was holding her throat. At first, she was going to call the police but decided not to since my dad left so quickly. Another chapter was written in my book of life. Another piece of a broken narrative.

3

Uprooted & Displaced

"When you are broken and neglect repair, everything and
everyone affiliated with you will not only feel the effects,
but will inherit some of your brokenness."
---Lucrecia Slater

*Even though the woman at the well was a native of Sychar, I wonder if
she felt displaced. I wonder if she felt as if she were a foreigner among her
own people. Her ways weren't ideal amongst the other Samaritan women
so she had been cut off from them and had grown accustomed to living and
doing life on her own. Isn't it funny how much distance sin and dysfunction
can put in between us and others and cause us to feel out of place?*

My mom decided not long after that incident that she "needed" to move
again. I suppose this was a way for her to try and recover and pick up the
pieces of her life. However, instead of recovering, she stayed wounded.
She decided to move us back into the home she was born in and grew up
in, the yellow house.

We called it the "yellow" house but technically, the house was gold.
Somehow yellow was declared the official color for it. My late great
grandfather built the house himself. From what I was told, that house was
the lively home, the social club home.

The pictures I saw of the house in its original state were gorgeous. It
was a radiant gold, almost the color of the sun. I suppose that was one
reason it was the popular house, because the color itself stood out in the
whole neighborhood. The yard was bordered with a chain link fence (I
wouldn't be caught with one now but no offense to those who still have

them) and was perfectly manicured with vibrant green grass.

Around the borders of the fence were pecan trees. My great grandmother was known for harvesting good tasting pecans. In the picture, I noticed another tree, my dogwood tree. At the time, it was only a young tree, barely recognizable as the big, strong tree I frequently climbed. A long walk way that lead to the front door, separated the yard in two down the middle.

On either side of the yard, also along the border, were lined some of the most beautiful azalea flowers I had ever seen. In hues of pinks, reds, and pinkish white, these flowers were definitely the show stoppers of the yard. There next to the side walk was another very large tree that produced some very large dark pink camellias. And in the corner of all this beauty, was a rock water fountain. I think the birds saw it more useful as their bath than a water fountain. They rapidly splashed in and out of the water daily, especially during the ridiculously hot Florida days.

But over the years, the warmth that filled the inside of the house and the beauty that captured the outside, slowly faded away. By the time we moved back, a lot of the beauty had disappeared. Black metal bars were added onto every window and door because of frequent break-ins by drug addicts. The grass was no longer plush and green. Instead, dirt took up most of the yard with speckles of grass here and there. The pecan trees still stood strong and yielded their nuts through the thick Spanish moss. And the flower trees, though they had thinned out, were still yielding bee-attracting flowers.

A year after moving back, my mother gave birth to my baby brother. His father stayed around a little bit. My mom was the abuser, unlike the other men she was in relationships with. He was very passive and he liked to touch me a lot. He used to always like to bounce me on his lap. And every time my mom saw that, she would go into a rage, from o to ten in 2.2 seconds. For the next year, this repetitive cycle continued in their relationship. He would do something to upset her and she would toss something at his head. I guess things finally came to a head one night (no pun intended).

I don't know exactly what happened, but this particular argument set my mom off and that was the last I saw my brother's father. As he ran like lightening through the house and out of the front door, a lamp flew out right behind him. If it hadn't have been for his cat-like reflexes, I'm pretty sure he would've ended up in the hospital with a concussion. His back was the last I ever saw of him.

One thing about my mom was that she didn't stay out of relationships for too long. She was a beautiful woman with an amazing smile. Her cheeks were high and rosy and she carried herself in a decent manner. After what was becoming a cycle of dead end relationships, my mom still longed for the right one, but she harbored and nursed a bunch of broken pieces. Her life was a series of dysfunctional chaos. What she showed on the outside was in stark contrast to what was on her inside.

Though she kept to herself, she always managed to attract the attention of another pursuer. There were a couple guys I thought were good for my mom. Guys that I actually liked being around, but for some reason, she quickly got turned off by them. It was almost like they were too "good" for her because it seemed like she was attracted to the

#coffeemoments
What we present on the outside can be very deceptive to the chaotic storms we harbor on the inside.

no-goods, the dead beats. Some were obviously no good. Others, hid it very well. My youngest sister's father did just that. It wasn't long before she would take on his last name in holy matrimony.

My mother married for the first time in 1989. This would be the first of several marriages. At first, he seemed okay. He was an Army veteran and had a regular 9-5 job. On the outside, things looked fine. My mom was pregnant with my youngest sister and seemed to be getting used to the married life-that was until her husband completely flipped the script and revealed his true colors.

My mom was in her third trimester of pregnancy when her husband attempted to end her life. Had not my "Bigmama" been there with her 40 caliber in her purse, I'm sure he would've succeeded.

Okay, before I go on, I must pause right here and reflect a bit. Let me tell you about this woman we called Bigmama. For those who grew up in the south, I'm pretty sure you had or have a Bigmama in your family. She wasn't like what we see on television, well she kind of was when I think back to those knee highs that seemed to always be rolled down to her ankles by the end of the day.

Her name was Rosa. She was the matriarch of the family and (in a very low voice I'm saying this) the best cook in the family. She was my great-grandmother and was my mother's grandmother. She raised my mom from birth up to her adult years.

Bigmama was a strong soul. One who didn't need the help of a man to do anything around her house. I don't mean this in a cruel way, I mean she literally didn't need a man to assist with much of anything. If she sought out help from one, you better believe she wasn't sitting on the porch sipping tea. She was right next to him getting dirty. And it didn't matter what it was, climbing the top of the house to fix a leak, laying cement (which to this day still bears the little footprints of us kids), laying sod, mowing her huge lawn, you name it, she did it. And she always found a way for us to be out in that huge yard with her doing something. She had hands the size of softball mitts. Bigmama loved working in her garden.

I credit her for spoiling me. Next door to the yellow house was a huge field Bigmama owned where she eventually built her home. We all took part in building it, along with a couple of her guy friends (more like senior pursuers). When the house was built, I spent a lot of time over there. It was cozy and yet, hate to say, near hoarder status. But I loved it, all the collectable antique dishes, photos, and trinkets. We had a ritual every time I either came over or stayed the night. We would make oatmeal, toast with butter and jelly, and a cup of coffee. Yes, I was drinking coffee when I was a little kid. Hence, my addiction to Starbucks!

Bigmama was a strong, independent woman whose work ethic was solid. After a long, tiresome day at work, Bigmama came home and changed out of her work uniform and right into some super old polyester pants, socks and knee highs with the pants cuffed inside, an old button up shirt, and a big sun hat. I hope you can grasp the image of this. She used to stand about 5'5", but over time she shrunk a bit due to osteoporosis and a rounding hump in her back.

She worked as "the help" literally. Long before the movie "The Help" came out, I got to witness it first hand in my great-grandmother's life. She worked for a wealthy Caucasian family. But unlike the movie/book with snooty families, this family were the sweetest group of people I had ever met. Throughout the summer and on some Saturdays, I went to work with her. The manicured yards and flower gardens were majestic. The neighborhood this family lived in and the hood I lived in were polar opposites.

Bigmama cleaned certain parts of the house on certain days. She prepared dinner for the family before they got home. After school or on weekends, Bigmama watched their only child, a daughter whom I became friends with.

On the weekends I went with her to work, I'd watch her look over her work. She stood in the living room, looked at me and stretched herself out real tall. Then she did a little shimmy dance and laughed that hearty laugh of hers. Giving her work one good look over, she gathered her things and we took off in her red Buick LaSabre, the longest car ever. I promise that thing was the Titanic on four wheels!

Back to that day we encountered my mom's husband. The day we arrived at home from church, he waited for us around the corner of the house. When he stepped from around the side of the house, in his hand was a large plumber's pipe. His eyes were red and wild. His demeanor was deranged and he kept pacing back and forth, telling my grandmother this had nothing to do with her, that "this" (whatever "this" was) was between him and my mother. Once Bigmama refused to back down and made it known she was carrying a gun in her purse, he hesitantly put the pipe down and slowly started backing away. We made it into the house and immediately called the police. Though my sister's father had already left, the police caught him based on our description of him. Once arrested, it was reported back to my mother that he was high on crack cocaine and if it hadn't have been for my grandmother's efforts, he would have surely killed her and attempted to kill us as well. She immediately filed for a divorce.

Even at the tender age of 9 years old, though I didn't know what to call it, I definitely knew something wasn't right about the guys my mom constantly chose to invite into her house and our lives. In the meantime, things were calm. Her divorce was finalized and she had not long ago given birth to my youngest sister. Just as she had done after the birth of my brother, my mom stayed home the first two years of my sister's life.

I took pride in being my youngest sister's oldest sibling. As young as I was, I took on the "parental" role to her. She was my baby, my daughter, my sister, my everything. I told my mom when she brought my sister home from the hospital that she was my baby. My mom didn't believe me, but I showed her.

My sister followed me wherever I went, mimicked my actions, ate the same foods as me, everything. Even when I caught a horrible case of chicken pox, that didn't keep my sister away. She slept with me and didn't get not one bump! That year (1991) had to be the worse spread of chicken pox. Just as the 5th graders were rounding up to go on a field trip to Washington, D. C., it had to be postponed. Too many kids were out with severe chicken pox. My sister soothed my terribly itchy skin by rubbing my back. She only knew what to do because she saw my mom's friend rub my back. While my chicken pox healed, my mom found a job. It was back off to work, she went. Working hard but hardly making any money.

Even while working, my mother received government assistance. Back in that day, it seemed like everybody was on government assistance. Did that little known fact stop me from being utterly embarrassed and humiliated every time we had to stand in those ridiculously long lines at the Human Resource Center? No, double no! I absolutely hated it.

Have you noticed for some reason, here lately today, food stamps have been on the come up? First, they're no longer distributed in books like they used to be back in the day. All benefits are put onto a card called an Electronic Benefits Card (EBT card). I've heard of people being just straight outrageous with some purchases. From gas to purchasing weave bundles, it seems as if people have learned to glorify government assistance. Well I didn't.

While I'm thankful the government was and can provide assistance to families who need financial help, for me, it always carried a stigma with it. Grocery stores seemed to know when folks received their food stamps. When my mom didn't receive her stamps, to Pic-n-Save, Save-A-Lot, Bent-n-Dent it was, but as soon as those fresh books of stamps hit her hand, we headed straight to Winn Dixie and Publix. Publix was the grocery store where named brand items were purchased and the cost was no issue to my mom because of the food stamps. I'm reminded of an episode of "Everybody Hates Chris" when Chris's family had to low budget shop because of low funds, but as soon as they received their stamps, to the name brand grocery store it was to buy name brand food items. It was a huge event.

It's so funny now, how I shop at Publix on a regular basis with my hard earned paycheck but I used to see this store as a privilege to be in since it was located on the Caucasian side of town. Funny.

Another place my mom treated us to, was a local bakery called Andrews Bakery. Because they were too expensive for my mom to afford with cash, she always waited until she received her food stamps to stop by. The family who owned the bakery were very friendly and knew who we were since we went there almost every month. Their sub sandwiches, donut holes, and twisted donuts were the absolute best. Move over Krispy Kreme, Andrews donuts had y'all for a while.

Having food stamps also meant my sister, brother, and me could take lunches from home to school. I hated being categorized as "free and reduced lunch" even though most of the other black kids were too. There was just something about being able to sit among other kids and feel like them with our little homemade lunches.

The bond between my youngest sister and I grew strong. I couldn't say that, however, about my brother and middle sister. Instead, a growing hatred (I use that word loosely) formed between my middle sister and my brother.

I guess the "territorial" trait kicked in. My sister hit, kicked, bit, and pulled on my brother every chance she got. This went on for years. I don't know if there was ever a quiet moment in that house due to fighting. Between either my sister and me fighting or my brother and sister fighting, there was constant noise. I never really fought with my brother. I did whoop his butt a few times though. Hey, I was left in charge, so that gave me the authority to whoop some butt and I did! Though we were some fighting kids, there was an unspoken understanding between my brother and me like no one else had in the house.

He was born with disabilities that kept him on "ten" (hyper) around the clock. At first, we all thought the boy was just plain old bad until he was tested for Attention Deficit Hyperactivity Disorder (ADHD) and Attention Deficit Disorder (ADD). He tested positive for both, which finally brought some clarity to why he was always wound up and it explained why he had a fetish with fire. The boy was a pyro, I tell you! Whenever he got a chance to get his hands on some fire source, he was setting something on fire. His toys, leaves, paper, clothes, his bed, yes, his bed! You name it, he stayed lit, literally! He was also very electronic savvy. He could disassemble any old electronic and reassemble it to where it either worked again or worked better than before he took it apart. But my brother was also very sensitive.

He desperately wanted a strong male figure in his life. This yearning caused him to cling on to every man that came into my mom's life. Almost constantly, I saw my brother's heart break time after time when the men decided to up and leave. My mom enrolled my brother into the "Big Brothers & Big Sisters" program hoping that would help him out some. Nope! Those people did the same thing as every other man did, either walked out of my brother's life or didn't show up at all. This messed him up. He became more aggressive and more destructive.

It didn't help that there were rotations of men in and out our home. Some stayed around for long periods of time, some very short. All the men who came around seemed to be after one, well three things from my mom: a roof over his head, food in his belly, and a good romp in the sheets. All of which were given to him with little to no effort or reciprocity. This was one of many lessons I was taught. *How to sell your value, worth, and dignity in exchange for time, attention, and a false sense of security.*

It wasn't long before I found myself starting to develop ill will towards my mother. At the time, I couldn't fully articulate why, I just knew I didn't like how she brought men over the way she did. If she wasn't at work, she was locked away in her room with the "man of the hour" and as always, left me in charge of my three other siblings.

#coffeemoments
Just because you do dirt behind closed doors doesn't mean that dirt doesn't have the ability to seep through the cracks and spew into the lives of other people.

After a while, I started snooping around her room...I waited until she left for work. Of course, I couldn't go in alone so I drug my partner in crime with me, my middle sister. I wanted to see what was so interesting about that room to keep her cooped up in there all the time. I guess curiosity killed the cat because I eventually found it.

We looked and looked and was about to leave when I noticed something up on the very top back of the shelf in the closet. I had to be around twelve years old and my sister, nine. We both took turns trying to jump up and open Pandora's box. Alas, we found a stool.

When we first grabbed the box, VCR covers fell out. All kinds of naked bodies and lewd positions and images filled our innocent eyes. We grimaced and "ewww'd" as we picked up and examined each movie cover. As my sister kept saying how disgusting that was, I felt a deep intrigue growing within me. The same one I felt when I saw my classmate pleasing herself.

We looked at each other trying to figure out if we should watch one of the tapes. And of course, you know what we did, we watched. I was caught up. I was engulfed in the images I saw on the screen. As mesmerized I was, I couldn't help but to think that my mom was doing these same things to the men she brought into her room. I felt disgusted and intrigued at the same time. I kind of felt icky watching, but I couldn't take my eyes off what I saw.

Before I ever became aware, that seed quickly took root into my soul. I became its slave. Every chance I got, I ran into the room and popped in a tape. The images were emblazoned into my mind, creating mental storage banks. The sad part about this whole thing is that my mother was never aware of the door she inadvertently opened.

I want to pause and reiterate a point that I will continue to stress throughout this book. I want to assure you that I am not trying to make my mother look bad in any way. I only reference her and others because they were origin points to my brokenness. Their stories are intertwined into my story. My mother, I'm sure, was unaware of her own brokenness. Her life was riddled with a series of unfortunate events that were the result of her own doing and maybe even inherited by her from her mother, my late grandmother, and her mother, my late great grandmother. It is important for us to understand that every root has an origin. It doesn't just appear and start to grow.

If that wasn't bad enough, my transition out of elementary school into middle school took a hard and painful nosedive. My mom met the man of *my* nightmares, Rob. He turned the charm-o-meter to the max every time he came around, trying hard to win us kids over. But there was something about him I didn't like. My 12-year-old intuition picked up on it and it stuck. My mom, however, was smitten. It was all about him, literally, to the point where he took our place, but there was a secret he kept that eventually reared its ugly head.

He wasn't appealing to the eyes at all, but he was a very smooth talker. His "mac" game was on point. What I mean by "mac" was, he could smooth talk his way into getting things he wanted. Not long after Rob and my mom started talking, he was moving his things in. Pump the doggone brakes! Yes, men came and stayed, hung around for a while and were in and out, but this guy moved *all* his belongings into our house! And I didn't like it one bit.

He drove trucks but his routes must have been local because he was home almost every night. And when he came home, he wreaked of alcohol and marijuana. It wasn't until later, I realized he had upped his drug game from weed to the hardcore stuff, crack cocaine.

I used to tell my mom that I didn't like Rob but obviously what I thought and said was irrelevant because here was this man who had a good job, good money, and showed interest in a woman with four children by four different men. Think she was letting him go? Not a chance. She even sealed the deal and slipped away and got married while we were at school. Yep. Just. Like. That. And you know I felt some type of way about that, right?

We all got home from school and I saw a ring on her finger. I knew I wasn't seeing things because that ring wasn't on her finger before I left that morning. Gravity took hold of my bottom jaw really quick as it hit the floor. They went to the courthouse to the Justice of the Peace. I was so mad I don't think I spoke to either one of them for a couple of days. How could she? She had already been married twice before that! And that feeling I couldn't shake about this man had gotten stronger. It wouldn't take long before he would confirm exactly what that feeling was.

On the days Rob didn't work or got off work early, he spent much of his time either lying on the sofa with a beer and the remote or locked away with my mom in her room. He always gave me this smirk every time he looked at me. The smirk was as to say, *"I got your momma on lock and there ain't nothing you can do about it!"* I just sucked my teeth and walked away from him. This wasn't typical behavior for me but towards this guy, I didn't even care.

My mom decided to pick me up from school one day. Though I didn't mind her picking me up to relieve me from the extreme Florida heat, I was utterly embarrassed by her car. As long as I can remember, my mom has never had a brand new car, let alone a decent car. This car was the epitome of a hoopty. It waited until she was right in front of my school to cut off, only for me and a few other people standing around, to have to push it to out of other people's way. Or it made a loud shotgun sounding, screeching noise as she rounded the corner. Just embarrassing.

I waited at the pick-up/drop off area at school when I noticed her car parked across the street from the school. I told my principal I saw her car so he would let me leave. As I trotted across the street and hopped in, my mom immediately looked away. I asked what was the matter with her. As she turned, that's when I saw it. The right side of her face, from her eye to her cheek, was swollen, discolored, and her lip was split.

I sat there in disbelief. I screamed, "Did he do this to you!? Ma, did Rob do this to you? He did, didn't he?!" Huge tears filled my eyes, distorting my mother's image. Instead of her admitting he did it or that she was finished with him, she only said, "He won't do it again. He said he was sorry." I was in shock. Sorry? Was she kidding me? Every dark image came to my mind of how I would murder him. I was an introvert and painfully shy, but I had a temper that easily ignited to 100 quickly. When I fought my sister and other boys, we fought to kill, well at least I did. And that was all what was on my mind at the time, to kill this dude who had put his hands on my mom. My thoughts reverted to my dad and my youngest sister's dad, who both also beat my mom. The rest of the ride home was silent, with me looking out of the window silently sobbing.

Many times, we as parents, aren't aware of the doors we open for all sorts of evil and spiritual strongholds to infiltrate our children's lives. I'm not saying that we must walk a tight rope and attempt to be perfect because we'll never achieve that feat. But what I am saying, is *we **must become more aware of what and who we bring around our children and/or what we expose them to.*** And unfortunately, many women have groomed this way of life as okay and normal. But what I've come to learn is that God never leaves a situation undone. Though things look bleak, He always finds use of it

#coffeemoments Looking back on the situation, I can see where my mom moved too fast. She never allowed herself time to recover and heal from other relationships. Just like the Samaritan woman lived in seclusion with her mess, so did my mom. She was helpless in what seemed like a hopeless situation.

4

Drawing from a Dry Well

"If you don't love yourself, it's impossible for you to love others. You can't give away what you don't have." ---Joyce Meyer

She continued pressing her way to that well every day at high noon. The time in which she went wasn't typical practice for the women of her culture. But because of her lifestyle, she had been casted out. She was deemed the black sheep of her group. Because women in her culture had maidens to assist them from drawing from the well early in the morning, I wonder if she ever felt lonely. I imagine because this was something she did on a regular basis, she had to develop tough skin and get used to the isolation. She had to get used to the stares, jeers, and even remarks from the others. And she trudged on, functioning completely in dysfunction.

You know, I think sometimes, well many times, we make vain attempts to draw from something that doesn't exist. We attempt to get love where love doesn't exist or it has been broken. We attempt to be nurtured where nurturing doesn't exist. We become so depleted until we go into overdraft to get what we so desperately crave for. That's what happened to me.

#coffeemoments We keep drawing and drawing, making withdrawals from an empty account.

Though I couldn't properly articulate it, I knew the mess I called my life wasn't right. I grew into a very insecure teenager with a growing addiction to pornography and a budding secret habit of masturbation. I was socially awkward and extremely shy. Warm affirmations and hugs and all that stuff that parents do to display their love to their children was nonexistent in my house.

While my mom was out either working or locked away in her room with Rob, I was put in charge of my two sisters and brother. I was responsible for cooking, bathing, and cleaning up behind them. At first, I was semi-okay with it since my mom worked so much. But after a while, I grew tired of doing it. After all, I wasn't their mother! But let me try to say that to her; I guarantee my teeth would've been out of my mouth and on the floor next to me.

Even though I disliked having to take care of those bad kids (yes, they were bad) who refused to listen to me, I did it because, well again, I didn't have a choice. And I knew when my mom got home she was always worn out. Her job wasn't ideal at all and wasn't even enough to barely sustain six people. And Rob refused to contribute anymore. So, knowing that, I reluctantly watched my siblings. Why couldn't Rob do it, you may ask? Because I didn't trust him, that's why. So as much as I didn't like the job, I did it to keep him away from me and us.

There were some occasions I went to work with my mom and kind of got a glimpse into her work world. Back in the day, minimum wage was around $4.25. She worked at hotels and motels, cleaning up behind some of the filthiest people I had ever seen in my life.

On days I didn't want to go to school, my mom said I could stay home (which wasn't often by the way) but that I wasn't going to sit at home and do nothing. So, she took me to work with her. Besides, I wasn't even trying to stay home with Rob, not in the least bit!

My mom wore a back brace because of all the bending down she had to do. Every day consisted of her pushing a cart full of cleaning supplies, fresh linens, and other room necessities.

During the few days I went to work with her, she had me go up the side of the hotel stairs to avoid being seen by management. Once inside, I looked around the room and saw stuff ranging from used condoms carelessly lying on the floor to severely stained sheets and trash everywhere. Without a word, my mom put on her gloves, tossed me a pair and we got to work. Long days at her job made me wish I had gone to school. But it was either hard work or constant bullying.

As I said earlier, I didn't like going to school. As a matter of fact, much of my school experience starting from middle school to high school graduation was horrific with trickles of good times somewhere in between. If I wasn't getting picked on daily, I was constantly worrying about my mom's safety on her days off at home with Rob. Where fun memories should have been forming and lasting friendships developing, that wasn't the case for me. And as if that wasn't enough on my already growing list of things to worry about, my girl parts kicked into activation (menstrual cycle).

We still lived in that old yellow house and I shared a room with my two sisters. For some reason that day, all of us were packed in that room, except for Rob. He was on the road. I think we were watching something on T.V. I was sitting on the floor when I suddenly felt a warm sensation up underneath me. I leaned on one side to see what it was and immediately got up and ran to the bathroom. I was terrified! My panties were soaked. I took everything off because I had bled through.

Wrapping myself in a towel, I walked back to my room and told my mom that I was bleeding from "down there" as I called it. I was confused. I didn't understand why I was bleeding. I immediately felt guilty because of my masturbating. I thought that somehow that had brought this on. My mom just turned and said "Chile, you got ya period! Don't *thank* that you grown! Ya behind betta not *thank* that you can go out and get pregnant! If I find out you done lost your virginity, you gettn' up outta my house!" All this spewed out of my mom's mouth in one breath.

My mind was spinning. Whoa! What just happened? I needed help. I needed to know what to do. And she didn't help me. I quietly walked across the room to my dresser drawer and grabbed some clean clothes. On my way back to the bathroom, I heard my middle sister say "Eww, you stank!" I locked myself in the bathroom and began sobbing. I looked at the bloody underwear in the sink and wondered why had this happened and how could I stop it from happening again. I cleaned myself up and wadded a bunch of toilet tissue in my panties to try to stop the bleeding. Still crying, I tried washing the stains out of my soiled panties. With no luck, I just threw them away. I sat on the toilet for a long time trying to figure out what to do. The tissue quickly started to soak through, so I had no choice but to face my mom again. I asked if I could please have something to control the bleeding. She reluctantly gave me a pad to put on and some to take to school the next day.

I was terrified to go to school like this. What if I bled through my panties? What if I bled through my clothes? Well, my worst nightmares came to reality because I bled through. My school schedule had just changed and I had health class. I was so happy that this horrible incident happened in this class.

My teacher was so nice. She was a retired nurse whose love for the medical field showed in how she taught her class. I wrapped my jacket around my waist and crept up to her desk. I explained what happened and she so kindly walked me to the back of the classroom. She handed me some pads and some other thing. It looked like a stick, but I later learned it was a tampon. My teacher also explained to me why my body responded in that manner. Since I had track practice after school, I told her I would stop back by and she could explain more to me. And she did, pulled out all her medical books and all. I decided not to tell my mom what I learned and the toiletries I received from my health teacher. Everything was totally awkward for me. My body was starting to change in ways I didn't understand. Biologically, I was developing into a young woman, but my appearance didn't show any proof of that.

I want you to picture this...don't laugh, just picture it. Okay, I know you're going to laugh but just get over it quickly. Alright, picture this, a skinny brown skinned girl, with a head full of thick, kinky hair, braces, hand me down, second-hand clothes and shoes, super flat chest, with a big backside unproportioned to the rest of her body. Do you have that picture in your mind? Okay, now picture that same girl getting shot down and picked on by almost anybody she passed in the hallways. Yep, that would be me.

I was socially awkward. I didn't know how to properly establish relationships with anybody because I didn't know what a healthy relationship looked like. No model of a healthy, even a halfway decent relationship was ever displayed in front of me. And I was severely shy and kept my head down most of the time I was in public. If I had my way, I would have never gone to school and subjected myself to daily bullying.

My favorite times of the year was when school was out for the summer (go figure) or at the end of every week when I asked my mom to take me to the public library. Aside from my awkwardness and terrible secrets, I loved reading, writing, and drawing. Going to the library away from the chaos of my hood and home, allowed me to do that without interruption. I stayed for hours either drawing Lion King characters or starting and finishing a book. I felt normal at the library. No one picked on me or cared about how I looked or what I had on. There I felt accepted. Too bad I was grossly rejected in school.

I was in the 8th grade with those hideous braces and drippy "Jheri curl." Let me pause right here and explain what a Jheri curl is. I have something even better, picture the movie "Coming to America." If you grew up in the 8o's then you know exactly what that movie is! One of the families in the movie were the creators of "Soul Glo" a curl activator. Better yet, just Google it and I'm sure you'll see exactly what a Jheri curl is.

So anyway, I was this awkward thirteen-year-old, extremely shy, with hand me down clothes and shoes on. And to top things off, according to my teachers and my grades, I was pretty smart (shouldn't be a bad thing but when you're an outcast it seems to be).

Having all those things going against me didn't help the way I saw myself at all. I had it engrained in my head that I was stupid and ugly. This came from validating the lies I accepted as my truth from my mother constantly and consistently calling me those things. An incident that happened in one of my classes put a final stamp on the way I saw myself.

In science class, oh my goodness, my teacher kept the thermostat set on the Arctic! Why he thought we were polar bears was beyond me. Even in the dead of summer in Florida, I carried a heavy jacket with me just for his class.

He grouped our desks together in fours. Across from me, sat one of the most popular girls in school. She always did things to get the attention of others around her. One of which was loudly pop gum that we weren't supposed to have in class. As she clearly ignored the teacher giving out instructions, I listened intently. Science happened to be one of my favorite subjects and we were preparing for an individual assignment worth a lot of points. Now the teacher said we had to work on this assignment alone, but uh.. *how*, when we were facing *each other* in groups of four?

Just as I started my work, I heard a faint "psst." I looked up and it was the popular girl. She mouthed if I could help her out (cheat) with her assignment. I was a bit taken aback but had a conversation in my mind that went something like this, *"Oh my goodness, she's talking to me! She's asking ME to help her with her work! I can't just tell her no. Maybe this is an opportunity for us to become friends."* So, I decided to slip her a piece of paper with all my answers on it. Being the nerd that I was, I knew the answers were correct so I smiled as I handed her the piece of paper, braces shining and sparkling everywhere. She said thanks and that I was "da bomb" (team 90's slang). Of course, I was on cloud nine by then. The very next day, however, that cloud was shot right from under me.

As I walked down the walkway to get to class, I saw the girl and a group of her friends standing around talking and laughing. As I approached, I smiled and was getting ready to speak to her. Before I could, she shifted her weight to one leg, sucked her teeth, and with a look of disgust on her face said, "Uh, Lucrecia, didn't you just wear that outfit on Monday? Today is Wednesday! Don't you have other clothes to wear? What, you poor?" Laughter erupted from her and her clique. Just like that, I had been humiliated in front of, what felt like, the entire school. Those who heard, chimed in on the laughter. Some said that was messed up. Others just stared trying to figure out what was going on. My face burned with embarrassment as I sped past those rude girls and into the nearest bathroom. I cried so hard and eventually lied to my teacher to allow me to go to the front office and call home because I was "sick."

After my mom came to get me, she must have fussed at me the whole way home. I guess her fussing was because I had let some girls talk about me and I didn't stand up for myself. I was so caught up in my thoughts that I didn't hear much of what she said. When we got home, I blew past Rob who, suddenly, always seemed to be home every time I got home (I later found out he got fired for being drunk on the job).

I ran to my room to change out of my school clothes. You know back in the day, it was almost blasphemy to play in your school clothes. That was one of the first things you better do when you stepped foot through the door, change your clothes and shoes. Nowadays, kids will go out in their brand new clothes and kicks to play in mud. Changes of the times, I tell ya.

So after I changed my clothes, I went outside and retreated into my favorite spot, a dogwood tree. This tree was everything to me, literally. It's almost as if it were a person. It was my place of therapy and reflection. During the spring, the dogwood yielded some of the prettiest white pinkish flowers and in the summer, the flowers withered but bright green leaves bloomed in their place. I used to climb almost to the top of this tree and perch up on my favorite branch. The branch was obviously worn down because of my frequent visits. For hours, I just sat daydreaming and thinking. Thinking about how my life would be different if we weren't poor. Why I had to wear second-hand clothes and shoes. Why couldn't we shop at regular stores like other people. What if I were another race. What if I had another mother. Why did Rob have to live with us. What if my father were actually around. I thought about him a lot.

After my therapy session was done in the tree, I slowly climbed down and went inside. My sisters and brother were doing their usual, fighting and yelling at each other. Rob would be grossly laying on the sofa like a rag doll with the remote in one hand and his other hand jammed down the front of his shorts, with a beer on the floor.

I ignored them all and walked into the dining room, another favorite spot of mine. And I either drew or read. I found that reading and drawing took me away from the chaos. They took me away from the reality of my surroundings. I could easily get lost in a book (remember my library tales). At the time, my favorites were R. L. Stine's "Goosebumps" series and Frances Hodgson Burnett's "The Secret Garden."

Looking back on my life then, I realize how chaotic things really were. The only peace I seemed to have was when I was immersed in a book, drawing, at the library, or in my tree.

I knew something wasn't right about the way we lived. One thing I have learned since being an adult is dysfunction is tricky. We may know that something isn't right but many times we tend to rest in the normalcy dysfunction brings. We can forever live a broken narrative under the radar if we don't catch it.

#coffeemoments
Deception will cause one to become blind to the obvious.

As I mentioned earlier, my siblings and I didn't receive hugs from our mother. We were hardly ever told that we were smart and would be and do great things when we got older. We put ourselves to bed at night. There were no bedtime stories or warm affirmations before we closed our eyes.

Instead, we were ridiculed daily. Beat daily. Yelled at daily. Put down daily.

Lived in fear daily. We learned to function on our own or was taught by the streets, school, or the dysfunction we saw at home.

Again, I want to make this known and clear. In no fashion am I trying to bring a bad light to my mother. I now understand that she couldn't give what she didn't have. She created lives in her brokenness and because she didn't recognize the signs and she accepted that narrative, dysfunction became her normal. However, it is my wish for people to see the trending patterns that flow from generation to generation.I'm reminded of a movie my youngest daughter loves, "Wreck-It-Ralph." I don't know how many of you have seen the movie, but after watching it repeatedly (at one point it was a permanent fixture on our DVR), I found it to be kind of a cute movie. One of the main characters in the movie is Vanellope von Schweetz. I promise she is one of the cutest animated characters I've seen. She's caught in limbo between video game worlds. She has accepted the story that because she's a glitch, she is trapped and can never leave the place she's in. Towards the end of the movie, the main character, Wreck It Ralph, realizes not only is she not a glitch, but she's the main character/ heroin in a video game. He sets out to show Vanellope this truth so she could begin to live out her truest identity. After some time, she no longer accepts the false narrative she validated for so long and begins to operate in who she was created to be.

I think many times, this is what happens to us. God makes it clear in His word who we are and how He created us to be, *"royal priests, God's very own possession"* (1 Peter 2:9, NLT), *"God's masterpiece"* (Ephesians 2:10), *"the apple of God's eye"* (Psalm 17:8; Zechariah 2:8), *"created in the image of God"* (Genesis 1:27). There are several other verses that confirm who we are, yet many of us have fallen short of this knowledge because we weren't exposed to it. Instead, we were exposed to the lies, facades, and pretenses. We became trapped by those lies and took them on to become our truth. And we began to function in that dysfunction. We began to live out the very results of those lies.

Sisters, we are NOT those lies that were spoken to us, over us, and about us. We are so much more than that. It's time that we closed our ears to what others have negatively said about us and open our ears to what our heavenly Father says about us. Because what He says is the truth and stands against ALL lies ever spoken and that will be spoken!

To do this however, we must be willing to go back to that little girl inside of us, show her and tell her this truth.

5

When Pretending Becomes Reality

"Don't allow your wounds to transform you into someone you are not."
---Paulo Coelho

The reality was, the Samaritan woman's life was a mess. She had been married five times and the man she was living with wasn't her husband. She was shunned by her own people, cast out to live and do life alone. Had she known that her wounds didn't define her, she probably wouldn't have allowed herself to grow accustomed to her lifestyle. She created masks that would create her reality.

Okay, so I'm not really a fan of magic, but the two magicians that captivated me are David Copperfield and David Blaine (ha, I just laughed because I just realized both of their names are David. I'm quirky like that). I remember growing up, I would be the first one to the television when I knew a David Copperfield show was airing. One of the shows I will never forget is when he made a Boeing 747 and an elephant disappear. To this day, I still don't know how he did that! And then there's David Blaine.

I believe I discovered him some years back. I couldn't even tell you what I was doing to catch him on television but I did. He was like no other magician I had ever seen. The incredible illusions he created were nothing less than indescribable. He seemed to thrive off the shock of his audience. They always tried to find a way to figure out how he did what he did. Some of the most memorable performances that are now emblazoned in my mind are when he submerged himself into water for I believe a week, pulled some sort of string out of his stomach, and froze himself in a huge block of ice for an extended period of time. Though all of David Blaine's performances were absolutely amazing **and** crazy, some were illusions, not real, pretend.

While the words pretend and illusion have slightly different meanings, they're still related. Let's call them cousins. They're cousins to

. Let me whip out a bit of Merriam-Webster for a minute because I really want to stress my point here in this chapter.

According to Merriam-Webster, pretend means *to give a false appearance of being, possessing, or performing 2a: to make believe: b: to claim, represent, or assert falsely.* Deception (deceive) means *the act of causing someone to accept as true or valid what is false or invalid.*

When we operate from a place of dysfunction, we tend to deceive ourselves. I Corinthians 3:18 (English Standard Version) says, *"Let no one deceive himself. If anyone among you thinks that he is wise in this age, let him become a fool that he may become wise."* But here's the catch, half of the time, we don't know we're even deceiving ourselves. Again, we're walking around and doing life **functionally dysfunctional.**

Have you ever created fantasies in your head? We all have, even if some don't want to admit it. We picture the perfect man, kids, home, life. While there's nothing wrong with a good imagination from time to time, where the danger comes in is when we bring what should be imaginary, into the realm of reality. We try to recreate fantasy to work the way we envision it. From a warped vantage point, we create these illusions of what we think our lives should be. That's what I did and from that moment on, a part of me died.

I was finally nearing the end of dreaded middle school years and about to transition into high school. With the very few girls I hung around, we talked and imagined how high school would be. What would the boys be like? Well, I didn't really imagine that, being that I was more of a boy repellant than magnet. The closest boys would come to me was to slap me on the behind. I had a small, muscular frame and a fairly large backside. What I thought, at first, to be "I'm digging you" slaps, I quickly realized that slapping my behind was only a form of bullying and a game for the boys.

You better believe, though, the last boy to slap me on the behind would never do it again as hard as I punched him in the face. And that was *after*

I chased him around the entire 8th grade breezeway. I may have been shy but I wasn't going to let anyone touch me and get away with it. Me defending myself came to great use as I had to fight off a creeper.

This day had to be borrowed straight from the pits of hell because of how hot it was. I had just gotten out of a long, grueling track training session and was tiredly walking home. My school was about 3 miles away from home. And I truly wished my mom had opted to come pick me up, instead she said I had to walk.

I was too tired and hot to put anything over my track tights so I just left them be and started home. The route I took made me feel a bit safe. On the right side of the sidewalk where I walked, was an old graveyard (I know, I get it, how in the world can I feel safe around a graveyard, one of the creepiest areas, right! But I felt safe). For some reason, my mom had a weird thing about cemeteries and she took us along with her on these creepy ventures just to look at headstones. On the left of the sidewalk was a main street and a neighborhood. I knew many of the older people who lived in the houses and I'd speak every time I saw them out.

As I neared the end of the cemetery, I must have been lost in thought or delirious from the heat because I didn't notice this bike pull up beside me. I jumped when an older boy came into my view. He had hopped off his bike and had a weird smirk on his face. Instantly, my heart started doing tumbles and back flips in my chest. Not from "oh my goodness, there's a boy trying to talk to me" vibe but an "oh my goodness, I do NOT know this boy! Never seen him before. I'm scared!" type of vibe.

Instantly, I gained some pep in my step. I didn't feel faint anymore. I walked in silence as the older boy coasted next to me on his bike. "What's ya name?" he asked in a husky voice. From the voice, I summed up he was a young man, not a boy. I remained silent. "Aye shawty, what's ya name?" he asked again. "I don't wanna talk..." croaked out of my parched lips as I walked faster.

Like a dog can sense fear, so did he. He hopped off his bike and started walking next to me. "Where you goin wit does cleats. Why you walkin' so fast? Slow down shawty!" The boy/man protested. Then out of nowhere, he slid his hand from his bike and onto my backside and gave a good squeeze. I jumped. I thought to myself, "dang why is there NOBODY outside right now?" as I franticly started looking around. No cars. No bodies. Not even a stray dog roamed the street. "Stop touching me!" I yelped as I swung my track spikes at him. He threw the bike down and grabbed me, this time painfully squeezing my behind. He tried dragging me in some bushes at the end of the road. I knew exactly what he wanted and I wasn't going to let him get it easy.

My experience fighting with boys came into play at that moment. I knuckled up and swung. I slung my track spikes around like a helicopter and started yelling as loud as I could. In an instant, the boy grabbed his bike, called me a nasty name, and pedaled off. I grabbed my backpack and quickly collected up all the contents that spilled out. I still had about another mile to go til I got home but I sprinted the entire way. Tears blurred my vision and I could hear people calling for me (*now* you wanna show up).

I reached the end of the dirt road my house was on. I saw my uncle's eighteen-wheeler rig sitting in front of the house so I knew he was there. I flew around the corner and through the makeshift wooden front gates that were attached to the chain linked fence and onto the patio. Nothing came out of my mouth but heavy breathing and sobs.

My mom was hanging some clothes up on the clothes line while my uncle talked to her when they both stopped what they were doing and rushed over to me. I told them what happened and my uncle immediately flew out of the yard. My mom wasn't too far behind him. They were going to go "on foot" looking for this boy. Reality set in quickly as my uncle turned around, hopped in his car with my mom close on his heels and sped off down the dirt road.

They never found him. Funny, years later, I found out that same boy turned man had been arrested and charged with aggravated sexual assault on some minor girls. When I learned of this, my heart went out to those young girls. And of course, thoughts flooded my mind, "how come nothing happened to me?" "Why was I spared?" All I can sum it up to, is it was God. His ways are far above ours. (Isaiah 55:8-9).

That ordeal sent my mind reeling in a direction that seemed uncontrollable. I secretly binged watched pornography, imagining that what was happening in the videos is what that boy wanted to do to me. Only against my will.

Summer time had finally ended. The creepy encounter with that boy was behind me and it was off to high school. I can't say that I was all that enthused about entering high school. I still had those dreaded braces and remnants of my Jheri curl still lingered. But whether I liked it or not, I was going to high school.

Vanguard High School is one of the older schools in Marion County. My mom attended and graduated from that school. She also attended my middle school, and lucky for me (inserts loads of sarcasm) I had one of her teachers in my 6th grade year! I know you're going "whaaaa!"" Because that's exactly what I did when I found out. And trust me, my teacher made it clear that he knew my mom and would tell her anything horrible I did. Which I don't know why he said that considering I was ridiculously shy. I digress. So anyway, my first day of high school came.

There I was standing at the bus drop off point on the side of the school. Several of the kids from my middle school were excited about being in high school, me on the other hand, not so much. The kids I saw there were monsters compared to the babies I attended middle school with. Full beards, deep, manly voices, extremely well-developed bodies, loads of cursing and foul language, and most shocking, pregnant girls.

I slowly walked down the hallway trying to navigate my way through the bodies of traffic. I was terrified. It seemed like every direction I turned there was a pregnant girl. I had only seen one other girl pregnant at my middle school and that was weird. But to see this as common and normal, was baffling.

For the first couple of weeks, I kept extremely close to myself, ha! I barely made eye contact with anyone and zipped my way through the crowds. Some of the girls I hung out with in middle school had transferred to another school. I had just one other friend at that time who transferred to high school with me, Shayla. And I clung to her for dear life, oh how I wish we had the same lunch period.

Lunch period was the worst for me. I kind of cringe now when I think about it, poor baby I was. The school was set up in the most unusual way. The center of the school was this massive round building that we all called, well, the round building and was surrounded by tons of portables and a few other buildings. It was two stories with a ginormous cafeteria smack at the center on the first floor. Our school was ridiculously huge so every lunch period seemed like the whole school was there at once.

Fights took place daily. I've seen fights in middle school. But these kids at high school fought like they were UFC fighters. They fought dirty and until someone drew blood. The hallway, I'm pretty sure, was laced with invisible drag marks of girls being "skull drug" up and down the walkway. Yeah, my school was a bit of a jungle at times.

While the jungle was taking place at school, an active volcano was brewing at home. My mom was still married to that monster, Rob. I promise I wished that man would vanish. I think the feelings I harbored for him came close to hate, tough statement I know, but very true. It was like a dark storm loomed over our lives with him around, as if our lives weren't already chaotic without him there.

My mom had some serious jokes because she used to throw out there that we refer to Rob as "dad." HA! If I wanted something outside of being bought with food stamps, she suggested that I call him dad and he would get it. I'd rather suffer or miss out on whatever it was I wanted. I had never, EVER called another man dad and I wasn't about to start then. And in my eyes, I knew he didn't deserve that title. There was something about Rob that I despised. It was something sinister about him. The abuse became outrageous, now extending from my mom to us. While I thought of the many ways I wanted to end Rob's life, my brother desperately tried to bring peace.

I think out of all this mess, my heart ached the most for my brother. He is my only brother on both my mom and biological father's side. As I mentioned earlier, my brother used to throw his heart heavily at the men who came into his life. With Rob, he tried, but Rob, instead of him just throwing it back, he squeezed the life out of my brother's heart. My brother would make comments about him wanting to play with Rob. Nothing. My brother would want to play video games with him. Nothing. After a while, my brother discovered a great friend in our dog, Brownie. That dog was everything to him. He was literally my brother's best friend, sometimes I think, his only friend. The older my brother got, the more I realized how misunderstood he was. Yes, he was a terror around the house and in school. Yes, he drove us crazy. Yes, he was dangerous at times (wielding a knife while chasing us around the house talking about he was going to kill us). Yes, he was all those things and then some. But at his core, he was a sensitive boy who wanted love and attention from a man.

At all our cores, we were sensitive children who yearned for the affections of our parents. Who wanted to be normal. We didn't want to live in a home that was infested with roaches, spiders, rats, and other dreadful creatures. We didn't want to almost daily be called stupid, ugly, retarded, and good for nothing. We wanted the physical abuse from our mother to stop. We wanted Rob out of our lives. We all ached. But we learned how to live with this. The truth couldn't show. We learned how to paint on the perfect masks. We learned our "yes ma'ams, no ma'ams, yes sirs, no sirs, please, and thank you's." We learned the art of illusions. We learned how to lock away the secrets that were killing us. Within the walls of our home, brewed some of the deadliest poison. But on the outside, people saw facades.

I wonder how hard it was for you or is for you to keep those things that nag deeply at your soul, a secret. How hard we try to present others with illusions. We present these false narratives to others hoping they would validate and accept it. We master the art of hypocrisy, like the Pharisees did when they tried confronting Jesus. They knew how to pretend well. They fooled everyone around them, but couldn't fool Jesus. He even said it! Matthew 23:25-28, NLT (Bible Gateway, 2015) *"What sorrow awaits you teachers of religious law and you Pharisees. Hypocrites! For you are so careful to clean the outside of the cup and the dish, but inside you are filthy—full of greed and self-indulgence! You blind Pharisee! First wash the inside of the cup and the dish, and then the outside will become clean, too. What sorrow awaits you teachers of religious law and you Pharisees. Hypocrites! For you are like whitewashed tombs—beautiful on the outside but filled on the inside with dead people's bones and all sorts of impurity. Outwardly you look like righteous people, but inwardly your hearts are filled with hypocrisy and lawlessness."*

Here's the kicker though, the things we hide have some tricks up its own sleeve because it always seems to manage to make its own appearance.

6

But the Truth is

"The truth is harder than a lie." – Francesca Battistelli

The truth was, the woman probably wasn't happy with her past and current situations. She had been married five times before and was at the time, living with a man who wasn't her husband. The woman probably may have just come to the resolve that this was the sum of her life. She had settled in the knowledge that her life was an epic fail. That was, until Jesus stepped right in the middle of her mess and completely changed the narrative.

I know by now, you're probably wondering why I chose the Samaritan woman to identify with. Well, because like her, I felt isolated by my past. I secluded myself in my own prison and instead of fighting my way for freedom, I too resolved that this was what my life had become. I learned how to pretend well. From my own creations and my mother's example. One of the most damaging things about deception is that usually by the time we start to open our eyes to reality, we've gotten too caught up. In too deep. Too late. But glory be to God, nothing is too late for Him.

The rubber was burning fast on that proverbial road. The truth about my mom's marriage was started to seep from up under the rug. She could no longer conceal the horrible realities of what took place behind closed doors. More bloody noses, busted lips, black and purple eyes, my anger grew inside of me as I looked on. There were multiple police visits. So many, I lost count. I distinctly remember one of the officer's words, "Mrs. Johnson, if you don't press charges and have your husband put away, he *will* kill you and there will be nothing more we can do." Those words echoed so loudly in my head, *"he will kill you"*. I couldn't do nothing more than sob and get enraged with hatred and anger.

And it didn't help that the part of the hood we lived in, everybody knew your business. There was always a main attraction every weekend. This drug house across the railroad tracks from my house was consistently the talk of the town. It got busted every weekend. But no matter the number of police raids and activity, it did not stop those drug traffickers from conducting business; they just became very smart with it.

I got so tired of my mom giving us sorry excuses for why she chose not to press charges and chose to remain with Rob. I didn't understand at the time, but now I understand. When we see no value in our lives and don't have a clue to who and whose we are, we settle. We settle because we've accepted the lie that "this" is the best we can do. We settle because we've resolved that no one else would want us because of x, y, & z. But that thinking and way of life was never God's intentions. Scriptures such as Ephesians 1:4 (NIV) prove that, *"For he chose us in him before the creation of the world to be holy and blameless in his sight."* Or this one, *"But God showed his great love for us by sending Christ to die for us while we were yet sinners,"* (Romans 5:8, NLT).

#coffeemoments
Self-sabotage can cause us to become blind to God's best and ignorant to our own existence.

It became hard for all of us to function properly in school. My grades suffered the most. Many days, I just coasted through class. When my friends asked what was wrong, I pasted on that smile and said, "nothing girl, I'm fine." I grew numb to my dysfunction.

Instead of turning to my usual nerve calming resources, my books, drawing, or my tree (yes, I still climbed it), I locked myself in the bathroom and masturbated. I wanted all the worrying, pressure, fear, chaos, everything to just disappear. And committing this sinful act was what did that, temporarily. It became my crutch. When I felt pressure, I retreated into the bathroom and just lock myself in there. I didn't realize how I had figuratively grew an umbilical cord from the emotional baggage to the sin.

Ephesians 4:22 (NLT) say, *"throw off your old sinful nature and your former way of life, which is corrupted by lust and deception."* There is something I want to highlight in that scripture. Our former way of life, or our sinful nature, is corrupted by lust and deception. Sometimes we can fool ourselves into thinking that what we're doing is right and if it's not right we try to justify it to make it right. That's how I treated masturbation, as a justification for me to release the stress I felt. Now, I wasn't saved at the time, well at least not the type of saved I've come to learn and understand now. So, I didn't understand the implications of my thinking. I mean, I went to church by means of the "drug ministry" (for the old schoolers who said their kids were NOT sitting up in the house while they went to church so the kids were drug to church, yeah that ministry). But little did I know that that very thing I justified was the very thing that was opening a door that would take several years to close back up.

I felt resentment growing in my heart towards my mom. Not only did she constantly choose to stay with Rob, but she chose him over us. We would see her go out of her way to ensure his needs were taken care of. When I told her I saw him bringing drugs (crack cocaine) in the house, she confronted him, but without an ounce of confidentiality. The night she told him, I hid in the dining room in a corner. That old house became pitch black once all lights were out and on the wall, was a very large antique mirror. If my mom's door was cracked, I could see in and hear. I know, I was horrible and nosey. I'm sure you have your share of stories too.

As she confronted him, she made known to him that I was the one who told her. I gasped and slapped my hand over my mouth as hard and fast as I could, hoping they didn't hear me. Did my ears hear that correctly?! My mom had ratted me out! To this man who was nothing to me. The resentment grew.

I went to bed crying my eyeballs out. I almost choked from holding in my sobs because I had to share a room with my two other sisters. I'm sure they wouldn't have heard me as hard as they both were snoring. But I held it in anyway. Bitterness burned in my chest. *"How could she, man?!"* was all that repeated in my mind.

A few days later at school, I got called into the counselor's office. Apparently, one of my teachers was concerned about me and talked to the counselor. Here came another mask. She asked how was everything going and she had noticed I was missing school and my grades were failing. I just fed her some lies and said I was fine and that I would do my best to bring everything back up. I slowly walked back to my class thinking why didn't I just tell her the truth.

Because the truth was, everything wasn't fine, nothing was. Our lights at home constantly got turned off. We barely had enough food to eat. Our clothes were severely used and second-hand. My mom was married to a monster who beat her senseless on a consistent basis. She had been admitted into a mental rehabilitation center after having a mental breakdown. She almost drove her and myself off a bridge, just wanting to end it all. Rob was trafficking drugs in and out our home. My siblings and I regularly hid in corners with knives waiting to pounce on him. I was afraid to go to sleep at night because I was afraid that last beat down from Rob was going to be the end of my mom's life. Why didn't I just relieve myself of all this worry and just tell the counselor? Because I still loved my mom enough to protect her from the heartbreak she would experience if Child Protective Services took us away. And I couldn't take the thought of being separated from my sisters and brother. So, the mask stayed on and the secrets stayed tucked away.

As if the day of sitting in the counselor's office wasn't enough, the dreadful night came. I knew something was up, I could just sense it. I sat in the den on the floor, watching the clock. The television was blaring but I couldn't even focus on what was on. I knew it was past my bed time, but I also knew that Rob hadn't made it home yet either. My soul stirred as I watched the time tick. My mom stood in the kitchen washing dishes, with that dusty, old pink robe on. She kept telling me to go to bed. I told her I was good and that I wanted to wait for her to finish cleaning up. Not sure if she sensed my anxiety but it was at an all-time high.

Ten o'clock rolled around and I still sat on the floor, in that same spot. My mom went into her room for something. I made a mad dash to the kitchen for the knife drawer. My great grandmother left a lot of her old items behind when she moved out and we moved in.

You know how everybody's house has that one junk drawer, well ours had at least six junk drawers. The one I dashed to had all old, severely rusted butcher knives. I pulled out the largest, most rusted one for myself. I also had my mom's gun tucked in the back of my shorts. She had given it to me, along with some bullets a while ago after Rob had beat her. He was going to die that night.

I knew the time had long passed that he should've been home. And I knew every time he came home late, he had the perfect opportunity to beat my mom. It was always too late when we woke up and made it to her room. He'd be out of the door again just as quickly as he came in. Well not that night. I was up.

I took several of the other knives out and ran and put them in my hiding spot in the corner of living room. The living room was considered the "nice" part of the house. It had all the plastic wrapped furniture (somebody please explain to me why the dag on hot plastic), antique pictures and fixtures. The living room was only a thruway. My mom tore us up if she thought we were in there playing. But it also served as a hiding place for my siblings and I whenever Rob came home. Sometimes we would catch him about to hit our mom, most of the time we didn't because we had to go to bed. I dropped the knives on the floor in the corner and went to get my siblings out of bed. They sleepily got up and went and sat in their places. They knew the drill. I gave each of them a knife and I sat down with them.

I heard my mom come back out of the room and into the kitchen again. My youngest sister whispered, "ma, I'm scared" to me. She called me "ma" all the time. I looked her in her five-year-old eyes and said "It's gonna be alright. Just be quiet." My other two siblings sat quietly, staring ahead with their weapons. Right then, the front door lock rattled. Rob was home.

He staggered through the darkness of the living room towards the kitchen. He obviously didn't even notice we were there by how intoxicated and high he was. He went right into the kitchen and stood next to my mom. Her back was turned towards us but I imagined her heart was racing out of her chest. I imagined how she tried to keep her breathing under control and maintain composure. Any wrong move and that could be it.

Rob stood menacingly over her, his over 6'2" frame seemed gigantic to her 5'6" frame. He asked for some money. "You know I don't get paid until next week. I don't have no money!" my mom protested as she continued washing the dishes. "I know you got something. Let me hold something!" Rob asked, more so demanded, again. My mom pleaded with him to stop asking for money she didn't have. In one swift move, Rob backed up, and his hand came down like fire across my mom's face. But he didn't stop there. He kept hitting and punching her. On cue, we jumped out of our places and charged at him.

He was surprised to see us still up and wielding weapons. I caught a glimpse of my mom leaning over the sink. Her eyes, nose, and lips were bloody. But she yelled for us to stop and to put the knives down. I had completely forgotten about the gun in my shorts. I wanted to cut him open. I saw red. Red from my mom's face and red from the built up rage inside me. My words exactly, "You touched my mama for the last time! I'm gonna gut you like a fish!" I screamed as I lunged towards him. He was really strong and whatever drug he was on that night gave him sub-human strength. He grabbed me by the neck and my sister by hers. He tossed her into the den and shoved me in between the wall and the refrigerator.

My younger siblings were crying and trying to defend us, but he pushed them too. My mom kept screaming and crying for him to stop but I guess whatever he was on had overtaken him because his attention was on getting us. My rage wasn't about to let him win. I wiggled out of the space he jammed me into and came out swinging that knife. The only explanation I have for why he didn't get not one cut and gutted was God had dispatched some angels around him. Because I was swinging hard and those swings were supposed to make contact. I kept screaming out through tears, "I'm gonna kill you! I hate you!" as I chased him through the house. He made his way back to the front porch, I guess when he realized that I really was trying to kill him. He dashed out of the door and down the sidewalk. I was still behind him, swinging and slashing my knife. With all the commotion, my great grandmother's lights came on in her house. She lived right next door to us. I'm not sure who had called the police but they too were rounding the corner. I was sweaty, hot, and disheveled. My siblings were standing in the front door crying as my great grandmother came to the house.

The police did their routine and asked loads of questions. All our knives were taken away but the gun still rested in the back of my shorts under my shirt. I sat on the front step staring blankly off into the night. Of course, nosey folks started gathering around, whispering and pointing. I sucked my teeth and shook my head. In my mind, we had become the laughing stock of the hood, even though half of the people who lived in the hood went through similar situations.

Bigmama consoled the little ones as I turned my attention to the officer questioning and almost chastising my mom. In that moment, I heard the greatest words uttered from her mouth, "I want to press charges." I jumped up and started balling my eyeballs out. Rob was going to go to jail. He was going to pay for what he had done and never return. WRONG! Dead wrong!

Yes, he got caught and was sent to prison on domestic violence charges, but my mom went every weekend to go see him. The white walls and clinging doors were just too much. Rob made more broken promises of how good he would treat my mom and us once he was out and how much he loved her and was sorry for all of what he had put her through. I refused to look at him through the glass window, even when he called my name. I just sat there shaking my head wondering why the heck I was there to begin with.

What I didn't understand at the time, was the amount of mind control the abuser has on the one being abused. The insecurities of the abuser transform and manifests itself as power and control and once he or she finds a weak vessel, they engulf that person. Though Rob was in prison, he still had power over my mom and it worked for a while. Until my mom started thinking again for herself.

Rob ended up doing a few years in prison. I guess reality settled into my mom's mind and she realized that a felon would do her no good, so she decided to divorce him. His papers were served to him while he was still locked up.

Statistics show that "On average, nearly 20 people per minute are physically abused by an intimate partner in the United States. During one year, this equates to more than 10 million men and women" (National Coalition Against Domestic Violence, 2010). Statistics also show that, "1 in 15 children are exposed to intimate partner violence each year, and 90% of these children are eyewitnesses to this violence" (National Coalition Against Domestic Violence, 2010).

Listen dear sisters, violence of any kind on the spectrum is dangerous whether that be physical, mental, emotional, or verbal. The danger meter is taken up several notches when children are involved. I watched my mother suffer at the hands of another human being for several years. I implore you to please flip to the back of this book and utilize the information provided if you or a loved one is involved in a violent relationship.

7

Blindsided

"Let those who are wise understand these things. Let those with discernment listen carefully. The paths of the Lord are true and right, and righteous people live by walking in them. But in those paths sinners stumble and fall."

---Hosea 14:9 (NLT)

The woman had no idea what she was in for when she showed up to the well. Her dysfunction became her norm. So, when Jesus showed up right in the middle of her mess, she wasn't ready. The scripture even records her actions, saying "the woman was surprised," (John 4:9, New Living Translation). She was surprised because Jesus had just disrupted the pattern. He had broken what was normal to her. But oh, how necessary it was for her to be blindsided.

The year went by fast. I had not long ago started the 10th grade and felt that I could finally breathe a little with Rob out of the picture, but not breathe too much. My mom was scarred by the trauma she endured by Rob and that trauma manifested itself through harsh verbal, emotional, and sometimes physical abuse. I disconnected. I had gotten used to being called ugly, stupid, a good for nothing just like "my no good daddy" as she always said. I had gotten used to being picked on by her because of my full lips, round nose, and big feet. I heard those things so much that they became a part of my view of myself. It seemed like my mom's dislike for me grew. I received the worst of everything. Okay, I gotta say that I believe a part of that had to be because I was the oldest. How many first-borns are reading this and can attest that the treatment you received was totally different than your younger siblings? I mean you saw those jokers get away with stuff your parents would've broken you off for. Just raise your hand, say amen, or head nod. I feel you girl.

Over the summer, I had finally gotten those dreaded braces removed and the rest of that curl cut out of my hair. My appearance drastically changed and it was apparent by the attention I received all a of sudden from the boys around the neighborhood and in school. And that attention was well received because I desperately yearned to be called beautiful. I desperately wanted to be pretty in somebody's eyes. I wanted so badly to experience what it felt like to be wanted and cared for and nurtured.

One of my mom's male friends came around frequently. He made it known that he wanted me and was willing to wait until I reached legal age to try to get me. For as long as I remember, he always talked about how beautiful my legs were and how juicy my lips were. I guess my mom thought he was playing because she never took it seriously. She always laughed and even called me his girlfriend.

While I was being outcasted by my mom, her male friend made sure to put me on a pedestal and above my siblings. In his eyes, I was the most beautiful and most desirable. I truly believe had the right opportunity been presented, he would have made a move. But you know what the funny thing was? Even though I thought he was totally gross because he was a grown man, in the back of my mind, I entertained it. I wore shorts slightly shorter when I knew he was coming around. I teased him just a little bit when he made comments about something on my body. I welcomed the comments because it fed the deficits in my soul.

My new appearance was something I had to get used to. I must say though; the timing of my changes was perfect. The movie, Clueless, had just hit the movie theaters and people everywhere were going crazy over it. Alicia Silverstone, Stacey Dash, and Brittney Murphy had all just given us life! Either the girls at school were running to Journey's to get the thigh high tights or the extra short tennis skirts and cute ruffle tops or the boys were wearing the sagging skater boy pants with the chains (well, some were). I quickly jumped on that bandwagon, I tried to anyway. Since my mom couldn't afford to shop at the mall or other retail stores, she bought stuff from Family Dollar or Pic-n-Save (oh my goodness, I have officially dated myself with that one!).

I distinctly remember rocking this one outfit, it was one of my favorites. It was a tan V-neck top with a tan and chocolate plaid wrap tennis "skort." For the millennials who may read this, for your information, a skort is a cross between a skirt and shorts. The skirt piece is either wrapped around in the front or it flaps over the shorts piece in the back. Dag, just Google it! And I wore these brown penny loafers with a chunky heel. At the time, Payless had good deals and good shoes. I had at least two other outfits like this one and even though I was still getting used to my new appearance, I loved the attention I received.

I thought since I looked different that I would try to step out of my shell a bit and try new things. I ran track in middle school and didn't exactly want to do that right away. I learned of a step team that was starting up and I thought I'd give it a try. My mom shot me down and said I was too scary to do it. Even though I was very scary, I still wanted to try out. I suppose she saw that I seriously wanted to do it so she took me to tryouts.

Tryouts were on an early Saturday morning. As we pulled into the high school parking lot, there were cars everywhere. Bass was rattling the car trunks. "Box" Chevys chameleon paint jobs and rims were glistening in the morning sunshine. The turnout was amazing, but terrifying at the same time. I had to try out in front of every eyeball there! My mom quickly sped off right after I shut the door. I slowly walked over to the crowd and lingered in the back. Some kids were yelling and chanting while others danced to the music. Relieved, I saw a few of my friends. I rushed over to them and relaxed a little. Montell Jordan's *"This is How We Do It"* thumped loud in cars, the mood was hype. Then the step master called for everybody's attention. She and some other girls were the ones who decided to start up a step team at our high school. They were pros at creating difficult steps and our try out steps weren't a piece of cake. The large turnout of kids was broken down by number and split into groups. In those group, we were taught the moves we had to audition with. An hour later, it was show time. One by one, it was like we were being lead to the slaughter house. My number came up and I went and stood as still as I could in front of the step master and her team of judges. Every nerve in my body was overreacting. When the music came on, I erupted into loud chants, heavy stomping, loud clapping and slapping of my thighs and feet. I did the step perfectly! This happened for all auditioning participants. After 3 hours of performances and deliberations, decisions were in hand. I made the cut! Besides running track, I never felt so accomplished before. Well, let me take that back. I won a young author's award in middle school for having one of the top fictional books (my gift for writing was apparent even then). I learned quickly, that being a part of a culture such as a step team, carried a reputation. Some on the step team were already well-known and popular, but others, including myself, weren't. We were the invisible ones before becoming part of the team. "Who is she?" "Oh, that's Lucrecia?" I became visible. I became somebody. I started getting noticed.

It wasn't long before my looks caught the eye of one of the most popular dudes at school. When I found out, I was shocked. I mean, yeah, I was on the step team and we did it big at every pep rally or event we performed at, but I mean this was a jock and he wanted to talk to me?! Besides, I had a "boyfriend" already. Okay, let me explain because I don't want to confuse you, chile.

So, remember earlier I mentioned me being a part of the drug ministry at church? Well, several of us kids were. And one of those boys started liking me and I liked him. I guess the reason why my mom didn't have a problem with it was because she was real cool with his parents. He was also a church boy. He didn't drink or smoke. He was on the high school football team and he played instruments at my church. But one thing he was known for was his voice. So, we kicked it for a while.

Because of our spiritual backgrounds, there wasn't much we could do, especially without an adult supervising us. I guess over time, I grew tired of that and wanted out of the relation (puppy love) ship. Of course, he was heartbroken and didn't understand why I was breaking up with him. I said it was because of his parents, they were too involved and I wanted more privacy. What on earth does a fifteen-year-old know about dog on privacy and her own business? Wow! Years later, I realized his parents had very little to do with me breaking up with him. It was the thrill of having the jock notice and like me. That was my motivation. But that was that. It was over. And then my sights set on the jock.

Things started off slow. He walked me to my class, carried my back pack, and we had small talk. Then he asked to take me to the movies. That was like asking if I wanted to die! My mom was all for my church boyfriend, and maybe even me talking to this new boy. But now we were talking on a whole other spectrum. One that she was *not* willing to cross over into. But the jock had charisma and charm. He eventually won my mom over and she agreed to let me go. Another shocker because my mom was overbearingly protective of me and my siblings, but especially me. I constantly heard threats about if I lied about having sex, she would take me to the doctor to get checked out and if it turned out I was having sex she would throw me out of the house. Or if I gave a boy my number, and he called, she picked up on the other line. Yeah, the muffled breathing kind of gave that one away. Or, I just got called all kinds of names just because, to make me feel lower about myself. So, her letting me go out was a huge deal.

We were going to see *Bad Boys*. Everybody at school talked about this movie. It was a spring/summer hit of 1996. All the popular kids were talking about it. If you were somebody, you were talking about this movie. The beginning of the date, I was terrified. I thought it would just be him and I on the date, but it turned out to be two other couples with us. One of the girls I recognized from school, the other one I didn't. I felt so inexperienced as the other girls carried on with their dates. They were hugging, kissing their dates and here I was stiff as a board with mine. As we settled into our seats, which happened to be the very top, back row in the theater, immediately the other two couples ravaged each other. Kissing, moaning, and groping was all around me. I sat looking at the movie screen trying to maintain my composure. Yes, I had seen this before on the porn videos I watched but that was in the comfort of my own secret space. My date looked over at me grinning. "You ain't never kissed before have you?" he asked. I tried so hard to act cool, y'all but I sucked miserably at it. "Yes!" I said as I sucked my teeth. You know what came next, "Prove it then," he whispered in my ear as I suddenly felt the warm moisture of his breath. Oh, my goodness. Was I really getting ready to do this? I didn't know what the heck I was doing. I was used to only pleasing myself with my secret sin. I had no clue how to interact with somebody else. Before too much time passed, he grabbed my face and shoved his tongue in my mouth. I was stunned, but quickly got the hang of it. So much for the movie. This had just turned into a make out session.

The jock and I dated for a few months before things turned up some notches. I went to his house often while his mother was either already gone or mysteriously "had to go somewhere." I now wonder if she knew what his intentions were with girls. Probably.

This particular evening, he tried urging me to have sex with him, I said no because I wasn't ready. He asked what did I mean I wasn't ready and I replied, "because I'm just not." I was very scared to respond the way I did because I didn't want him to break up with me. I guess he was used to getting what he wanted because all of a sudden, his mood changed and he was ready to take me home. It was around eight that night when he pulled up in front of my house. Before I got out, we sat for a few minutes talking in his car. I could see my mom's room light on so I know she was either in the room or her bathroom. I sat and listened as my boyfriend explained how much he cared for me. Then he uttered these three words. The three words that lifted all restraints and erased all boundaries. He said, "I love you." I felt like the wind had been sucked out of me. Did he really just say that? I felt my heart flutter so hard with overwhelming excitement. He loved me! Somebody loved me! I smiled and asked, "for real?" Ladies, why do we do that? Why do we play cute with empty questions like that? He said yes and leaned in and deeply kissed me. He said he wanted me and the floodgate of affirmations flew out of his mouth. Anything to get my panties down, he said. "You mean so much to me," "you are beautiful," "I will never hurt you," "you are so special." He went on and on, though he had me at "I love you." So right there, in front of my house, as I climbed into the back of his car and removed my pants and panties, I gave myself to him.

Contrary to what I watched on the porn videos or those steamy late night HBO movies, there was nothing pleasurable about that moment. I felt like fire was tearing my insides out. As he moaned with pleasure, I moaned with pain. The more he moved the more I wanted him to stop. But I suppose he reached his climax because he violently shook for a moment and then flopped on my chest. It was over. Just like that. As quickly as it started it was done. My body was riddled in pain. Then I felt a gush of warmth flowing from in between my legs. What in the world? As I reached my hand down to investigate and pulled it up into the streetlight, I saw crimson. Oh no, I was bleeding! My boyfriend saw my hand, said a few curse words, and handed me some wipes. Some wipes? I see somebody was prepared (inserts loads of hindsight 20/20 sarcasm).

I quickly but delicately cleaned myself up and stuffed the soiled wipes in my purse. My boyfriend readjusted himself back into the front seat. Since I was in so much pain, I slid out of the back car door and back into the front seat with him. Quietness seemed to engulf us forever until he broke the silence. "Well, I gotta get going," he said as he leaned over and gave me a kiss on the cheek. I smiled and said okay and that I loved him. He said he loved me back as I got out. I stood for a second as he pulled off, replaying what had just happened over and over in my mind. "I gotta tell my sister!" I thought. She was younger than me, but because I didn't have anyone else to talk to and was scared to death to talk to my mom, she was my confidant. I slowly walked in the house because I was still in so much pain. But I had to play it normal. My mom had seven senses it seemed like. The slightest shift in my mood, she always assumed the worst. One time, I had a pounding headache. She assumed that I was pregnant. I know, I'm shaking my head too, still going, "whaaa?"

As I walked through the front porch and living room, I could hear my mom's television on in her room. She knew I was coming back home around this time, so her hearing me didn't alarm her. I stood in the doorway of mine and my two sisters' room. My youngest sister must've been somewhere with my brother because only my middle sister was in the room. I rushed over to the bed and told her what happened. She, in such an overdramatic tone, shouted, "so, you and him hunched? Like what we see in those videos? Eww! How was it? What did it feel like?" I half laughed and half told her to shut up and quiet down because she knew our mom had dog ears. After I filled her in, we both got ready for bed. As the night went on and the old house creaked and settled, my mind was flooded with the events from earlier and those three words, "I love you." I smiled to myself and a shiver of excitement flooded over me. I couldn't wait to see him.

A few days passed and I hadn't seen my boyfriend. I couldn't reach him by phone either. At school, as I walked to my usual spot with my friends, I had an odd feeling. Every time I passed a group of boys, I heard snickers and whispers. I found it weird but didn't pay it any attention, at first. After this kept happening for about a week, I couldn't help but think that the boys somehow knew what I had done. "Nah, he wouldn't do that to me," I nervously thought to myself. But why hadn't I seen him around and why hadn't he called me yet? My friends all asked the same questions, although they had no idea what I had done. I lied to cover for him and me and just said he was sick. I eventually ended up seeing him back at school.

Trying to play it cool, I walked over to him and grabbed his hand, very excited and a little bit upset to see him. His mood was different towards me. He took his hand away from me and said he had to get to class. Funny, because I didn't hear the bell ring. The rest of the day I sat wondering what in the world was up with him. When I got home, I wasn't really in the mood to talk, so I was happy to find the house empty. Everything was in its usual dusty, torn up place. No matter how much we cleaned that house, it still looked and smelled horrible. With its super worn down furniture, old moldy carpet, and extra critters wandering around, there was just no hope. I grabbed a VCR tape off the top of the television and popped it into the VCR. *Dangerous Minds* was one of my favorite movies, but at the time it was depressing me more. I went into the kitchen and grabbed the phone to call my boyfriend. No answer. Dang, I thought, what was really going on?

The weekend quickly came. This was a huge weekend for me because the step team was performing for the city. Though I really wasn't in the mood to perform, I got ready anyway. My sisters, brother, and mom had already walked up to the auditorium to get in on the events. As I had just finished putting my outfit on, my middle sister busted through the front door panting and sweating. Alarmed, I screamed, "girl, what's wrong with you? Somebody chasing you?" as I looked out of the door. "No!" she managed to get out. "Your boyfriend up there with some other girl!" Wait, what? Let's pump some brakes and put this thing in reverse so I can hear that again. I asked her to run back what she had just said and she repeated exactly what she said with the smart comment, "you heard me!" I felt like I was in a time warp. Then my mind went back to the times he acted weird around me or avoided me altogether. It was because he was with another girl. My sister stood and watched me hard for my reaction. Though I tried playing it off, she could see right through the act. I was disillusioned into thinking that he loved me. I mean, that's what he said. And I gave myself to him, I endured the pain of giving myself to him because he loved me, or at least that's what I thought. I wasn't prepared for this blindside blow my sister had just inflicted.

How many times has this happened to you? You gave your heart to someone, only for it to be broken by betrayal. Remember our woman at the well? She went through five marriages and had again settled for someone who hadn't yet committed himself to her. But why? Why the repetitious cycle of the same dead-end relationships? One reason is because of the law of attraction. We attract what we give off. Another reason is because of the things that stemmed from our childhood. From the age of 3 to 15, I had been schooled on what dysfunctional relationships looked like. I had continued the cycle my mother started.

#coffeemoments

If we aren't careful to catch, pull up, and destroy those roots from early parts of our lives, they can, will, and do wreak havoc in our lives to come.

8

Unbreak My Heart

"I can be changed by what happens to me. But I refuse to be reduced by it." ---Maya Angelou

It wasn't clear as to whether or not the woman's heart had been broken.

But if I had to guess, I'd say it had since she had been married five times. She had an impression of what love was, but it was clear that that impression was distorted. I wonder where the origin of that distorted view of love came from? Was it a root from her childhood that had grown into a ghastly tree of emotional chaos in adulthood? That's where Jesus met her, right in the middle of her distorted perspectives. His mission was to unbreak her heart, heal her, restore her, and introduce her to love, Him.

They say time heals all wounds, but I beg to differ. What time did for me was only give me opportunities to revisit and ponder on old, painful memories. Every time I thought of an old memory of my ex-boyfriend, I developed a thought process. The process went something like this, *"he hurt me, so I will hurt them. I will never again let what happened to me, happen again!"* The *"them"* I referred to were all the male pursuers in my life. I was riddled with invisible stab wounds from the men in my life, ranging from my ghost father to the boy I gave my purity to. My mindset went savage, fast. I did to guys what they seemed to love doing to us ladies, woo us, take advantage of us, and leave us on the side like yesterday's garbage.

I went through the rest of high school dogging boys out. I used what rested in between my legs as a weapon instead of a sacred treasure God intended it to be. My relationships with guys never lasted long because in the back of my mind, they only wanted to hurt me. But I was sure to cut things off with them first before they had a chance to cut me off. I gave them what they wanted, but only on my terms. I had the mentality of a verse in Beyoncé's song, *Independent Women*, *"when it's all over please get up and leave."* Little did I know I was creating a monster (within myself) out of my antics.

I had since gotten my driver's license and my mom made me take her to work. Since she worked the 2nd shift, that meant I had the whole evening to myself. Well, of course there were my sisters and brother. My middle sister learned the art of gold digging. She had at least three dudes lined up ready to use them up for their money. There were always guys at our house. She was only 14 years old! My youngest sister and brother were just down for whatever. They enjoyed our joy rides around town when I dropped my mom off at work. Though I told myself that guys would only be seen as objects to my satisfaction, I ended up going back on my word a bit, well a lot.

I met this guy in school; he was a year older than me. It wasn't long before he and I were an item. I handled the relationship with caution because I knew who I was dealing with, another jock. He had the looks, was very well known, and was a top football player. I had already been scarred by a jock before, I wasn't about to let this one do the same. My mom had suspicions about my activities. She constantly questioned what I was doing and where I had been. Okay, yes, I was very, very sneaky, but I didn't disrespect my mom to her face. I wasn't that bold. As I mentioned earlier, my mom was crazy. Like Bill Cosby famously said in his television show, The Cosby Show, "I brought you in this world and I'll take you out!" Yeah, my mom meant every word.

This guy was very different than my ex-boyfriend or any other guy I interacted with. He was very gentle with me and my feelings. He was actually digging me. Kids at school thought we made a cute couple. I was happy to finally be with someone I thought loved me. We spent a lot of time together. My mom wasn't too thrilled about him coming over, so when I'd take her to work, I went over to his place. His mom was very nice and welcoming to me. It wasn't long before he and I took our relationship to the next level, we started having sex. We had sex a lot, some protected, some unprotected. I started to believe in my heart that he was the one, the one that I would eventually marry one day. I want to pause right here.

Okay, so your girl is about to go into medical mode for a hot minute, so stay with me. In science, the term used for an irregular heart beat is called an arrhythmia. The feeling is usually described as anything from skipping a beat to fluttering. Research says that arrhythmias can range anywhere from harmless to dangerous. The key though, is to get it checked out anyway. Because what may seem like nothing can indeed be deceptive and turn dangerous. Do you see where I'm going with this? In my heart, I felt like this guy was it. He was the real deal. He made my heart flutter, but as Jeremiah 17:9 (New Living Translation) says, *"The human heart is the most deceitful of all things, and desperately wicked. Who really knows how bad it is?"* If we're not careful to pay close attention to rhythms of our heart, we are sure to set ourselves up for the trap. Proverbs 4:23 (God's Word Translation) says, *"Guard your heart more than anything else, because the source of your life flows from it." Okay, I'm off my science soapbox. Irregular heartbeats can be deceptive and lead our minds down a dangerous path.*

I talked to one of my good friends all the time about him. She had recently started dating my boyfriend's best friend. Though we never went out together outside of school, we all always hung out at school.

Graduation was nearing and we started hearing buzz about a hotel party for the seniors. My friend and I were both in the 11th grade and wanted to go to that party so bad, but we knew our moms were not having it, so we had to formulate a plan.

The plan was to create a date night and say we were all going to see the movie, *"I'm Bout It,"* but to really head out to this hotel party. I was so hyped and excited. I knew the plan would work perfectly because my mom worked 2nd shift and when she got off work, she usually went straight to her boyfriend's house. Yep, after she picked up the pieces of her life, she started dating again. The man she chose was several years older than she was. He was nice but I had to ask why such an age difference (okay aside from all the adjectives, he was twenty-two years older than she was). She said she loved him, so what could I say? Since she was back on the dating scene, that meant I was back on babysitting duty. Two nights before, I asked my sister to watch our younger siblings. I explained the plan to her so in case something went wrong, she'd be able to quickly contact me. My plan was solid.

My boyfriend came around the time my mom got ready to leave for work. She questioned the mess out of us and started making threatening comments to me about getting pregnant or doing something stupid. I told her I wouldn't (lies).

In my purse, I stuffed some changing clothes to party in when we got to the hotel. We left out and my boyfriend walked over to the passenger side of his car. He opened it and helped me in. Y'all I had never seen this in action; a man opening a door for a woman. I was over the moon. When he got into the car, he let out a loud breath of relief. He knew of the plans my friend and I had made to be with our boos that night.

We rode down the highway talking, laughing, and holding hands. About twenty-five minutes later, we arrived at the hotel, the Marriot. I anticipated walking into a room filled with other young people, loud music, and fun. Instead, when my boyfriend opened the door to the room, there was one other couple in there. I didn't know them and they looked a bit older than my boyfriend and me. He knew them and dabbed the guy up.

There was a spread of alcohol on a table and Adina Howard's *"Freak Like Me"* was playing. I looked at my boyfriend and tried giving eye signals as to what the heck was going on. I didn't want to seem so "young" or inexperienced but I really wanted to know what was going on. He caught on to my eye signals and walked next to me and placed his arm around me. He whispered in my ear that everything was cool and for me to relax. I instantly got a sickening, heavy feeling in the pit of my stomach. Something wasn't right, something was about to go down.

The night went on and the couple made their way to the bed and started getting it on under the covers. While I looked in disbelief, my boyfriend looked at me like what was I waiting on. He was ready to get it on too. I was well accustomed to watching sexual acts displayed on pornographic videos in the privacy of my own residence. Of course, I engaged in my own sexual activities in private, but to see it happen before my eyes was something different.

The two carried on as if we weren't even in the room. I guess my boyfriend saw my discomfort and he sat over on the other bed and patted for me to sit next to him. We sat facing the door and softly talked a bit. Either the music flooded out the noise of the couple or I had somehow managed to drown it out. We finally laid down in the bed and talked more. I knew what he wanted to do, but I was way too uncomfortable to do anything. He asked if I wanted to go home because he didn't want to force me to stay. On one hand, I did want to leave because I was very uncomfortable but on the other hand I didn't want to seem weak. I asked my boyfriend if he knew about any of this before we got to the hotel, because again, this was supposed to be a party. He claimed he didn't, but his actions seemed suspicious. And where was my friend? She told me she and her boyfriend were down and were going to meet us at the hotel. Why wasn't she there? Even though my antennas were up and fully alert, I told my boyfriend I would just stay and try to sleep through those two tearing each other up next to us.

It was close to 1am when the phone inside the room rang. I must've been in a deep sleep because the sound of the phone startled me. My boyfriend picked the phone up since he was the closest. He said it was for me and passed the phone to me. For me? Nobody knew I was there except my friend and my sister! That feeling I had as I watched that couple having sex in front of me, yeah it came back but twenty times worse.

I answered the phone and my sister just let it out. "Crecia, you need to come home NOW! Ma ended up coming home early from work! She questioned me asking where you were and I told her I didn't know but she knew I knew something! Crecia you need to get your behind home NOW! They out looking for you!" I was terrified. As she talked, I saw my sixteen-year-old life flash before my eyes. I knew it was over, my life that was. I asked my sister if she told our mom what hotel I was at. She said she'd forgotten the name of it so she told her the Hilton.

I hadn't prayed so hard before in my life. I started praying for God's covering. I started pleading the blood. I prayed that if He spared me from the murdering hands of my mom that I would give up pornography and masturbation and that I'd keep my legs closed until I got married. You know how it is y'all. We know we've gotten caught up in the worst of situations and it was going down and we pray and ask God to take it all away. We make all these broken promises to God as if that's going to make Him budge. His grace is truly sufficient and it covers us when we make stupid decisions.

I immediately woke my boyfriend up and told him we had to go. Now. He asked what was going on and after I explained, he was fully awake. He hopped out of bed, put his clothes back on and we were out the door. The whole ride back, my stomach was in knots. I couldn't think of anything else beyond how many times and the many ways I was going to die. My boyfriend drove in total silence, his eyes focused on the road. He was scared for me.

We finally ended up on the dirt road to my house. It looked extra dark that night and I felt like I was being lead to the slaughter. The railroad tracks in front of my house reflected the full moon's glow, making the road look even creepier. As we got closer to my house, I could see the silhouette of my mom's boyfriend's black truck. It sat facing our direction so if anyone was inside the truck, they knew right away it was us pulling up.

My boyfriend's car stopped beside the truck as we quickly and fearfully looked at each other. He and I got out of the car at the same time my mom and her boyfriend were exiting the truck. My boyfriend immediately started apologizing and tried to explain. I don't think any other words came out of my mom's mouth besides curse words. Her boyfriend went over to my boyfriend and said something inaudible. Whatever he said must have scared the daylights out of my boyfriend because he quickly ran back to his car, hopped in, and sped off. Literally left me in the dust.

Without hesitation, my mom immediately grabbed me by my shirt and yanked hard. She slapped me in the face, calling me several inappropriate names. My middle sister came to the door and started screaming for her to stop. That did nothing but make my mom even madder.

The next couple of weeks were horrible. My mom switched her hours to day shift so she would be home when we got in from school. Every day she got in from work, she either cursed me out or slapped me around. One day was the worst of them all.

Now, I've been beat badly before by my mom. To the point she drew blood. She used to beat us with whatever was in her hand or near her. If all that was near was a can of vegetables, she threw it. But this day, was different. Her anger directed towards me had kindled for some time.

I heard her come through the door. I tried to act normal but braced myself for the worst. My middle sister was in the kitchen and my siblings were in their rooms. I heard my mom put her purse and keys down as she neared the doorway to the den.

The minute she stepped through the door, her eyes locked on me. Something obscene came from her mouth as she flew over to me and jumped in the chair I was sitting in. She grabbed me by the throat and started yelling curse words at me. She called me all kinds of ho's and whores and words I wouldn't dare repeat. I screamed as I tried pulling her hands from around my neck.

My sister came to my aid and jumped on my mom's back to try to get her to let me go. All the anger that built up over time came to a head in that moment. Like a volcano erupting, my mom let it out on my sister too. She slung her across the den and jumped back on me.

I cried so hard, my eyes felt like they were going to pop out of my head. I understood the wrong I had done, but did it deserve this? Nobody saw the hell we went through behind the doors of that house. The anger that came out of my mom was from more than what I had done. She unleashed on to me everything she had been holding on to throughout her entire life. The broken relationships, the abuse, the trauma, the neglect and abandonment. All of it came out on me. I refused to hit my mom. I tried my hardest to keep from defending myself in that manner. She grabbed me by my throat again and squeezed. This time I had to put my hands on her because I was losing my ability to breathe. I pushed her off me and fell back into the chair. I held my throat and sobbed. My mom was crying too, because she was still angry and hurt. She finally left the den and went into her room, slamming the door hard behind her. My younger siblings were bystanders to the whole thing. They stood by quietly and looked at me with sad eyes. I got up out of the chair and slowly walked past them and outside. I climbed up into my tree and sat there until night fall.

My heart ached. It hurt beyond words. My boyfriend, I'm sure, had broken up with me, my mom hated me and I was alone.

#coffeemoments
If we aren't careful and are led by our hearts, we can end up on a painful, sometimes dangerous path.

Our hearts, as the Bible heavily refers to, isn't the organ in our chests, but rather the center of who we are. It's our core, motivations, intentions, emotions, and thoughts. The Bible is clear as to why we're to guard our heart, because it's deceptive. So many of us end up in dead end and dangerous situations because we aren't careful about who we give our hearts to.

Like the woman at the well, we seek fulfillment from something or someone that's empty, that and who could never fill the void in our souls. We desperately try to make good of our dysfunction. So instead of seeking treatment, we continue re-injuring that wound repeatedly. Until we're fully depleted and broken.

9

Forward March

"When the path reveals itself, follow it." –Cheryl Strayed

Jesus wasted no time with His mission. He knew He had to have a divine meeting with this woman. Though her life was in shambles, it was orchestrated so she could meet Jesus at the perfect time and be transformed. To her, walking to that well was just like any other day. The same pathway, same bucket, same stares and whispers. But to Jesus, it was the day a woman's broken pieces were going to be mended back together. Not just her, but an entire village was about to be transformed.

It felt like an eternity being grounded (or on punishment as African Americans call it). My relationship with my mother was strained to the max. All the times before when she verbally and physically abused me weren't anything compared to the mental torment she inflicted onto me. It had been months since the incident happened with my ex-boyfriend, but my mom always felt the need to bring it back up. Day after day, I was either being called an inappropriate name or being kept from society except for school. I longed for the day I graduated. The thought of going to college was far-fetched considering my grades weren't the best and my mom didn't have the money to pay for college. And my father was out of the picture so that definitely wasn't an option. Yet, I had my mind set on leaving home, so I was going to college, one way or another.

My senior year of high school didn't start off the greatest. I was still grounded from what happened my junior year. I know right! Not long after school started, I signed up for the Future Business Leaders of America program (FBLA) and loved it. The teacher taught us corporate world skills and how to land a good job. I didn't have any social etiquette beyond the manners my mom and great grandmother taught me when I was younger and I knew how to pay bills and lie to bill collectors when they called. My mom used to send my little 7-year-old self into various companies with money wrapped up in a note to pay the bill. I could barely see over the counter and would just slide everything under the glass window. So, taking this class was exciting for me. It's where my love for typing was born.

My mom wasn't too thrilled about all the activities I was involved in with this program. I had to go to conferences, not an option because they were a part of my grade. There were only two conferences I was allowed to go to and that was because they both counted as large percentages of my grade.

#coffeemoments
We inflict onto them
our brokenness and
make it their burden
to now carry.

Looking back now, I can see where her insecurities attempted to rule my life. And for a long time, they did. When we are in a depleted place within ourselves and don't know who we are, we tend to, either consciously or unconsciously, wear the people around us down.

It wasn't long before I landed what I thought was my dream job working at the Marion County Courthouse. My dream was to work for the FBI or NSA so to work in the courthouse was a good step in the right direction. I fell in love with criminal justice through my Criminal Justice teacher, Mr. Miller. He was a retired agent and his love for his career came out through his teaching. He showed us the movie, *Se7ven*, and that sealed the deal for me. Of course, we had to get written permission from our parents to watch that movie in school. Now that I think about it, that movie was way too gruesome for a bunch of teens to watch in school, but anyway, I knew without a doubt I was going to go to college and get a degree in Criminal Justice. I didn't know how on earth that looked considering again, we were dirt poor but I was determined to find a way and the way presented itself and changed my life forever.

My homegirl and I were posted up on the wall during lunch when we saw these men walking through the hallway with these weird uniforms on. They were fine (emphasis on fine). Fresh, clean haircuts, buffed, tall, dark, and did I say fine? We watched on in awe and curiosity as girls flocked all over them. The thirst was real y'all. My girl and I didn't approach them but they piqued our interest.

The next day, the guys were back, this time in different uniforms. I recognized who they were this time. They were soldiers. They were in the Army and were called recruiters. They were on a mission, looking to recruit some fresh meat. This time, my homegirl and I approached them. Okay, I'll admit, we became a little bit thirsty too. I mean, geesh, these guys looked like they came out of GQ magazine. I'm sure we looked absolutely ridiculous to them. Us, young girls, throwing ourselves at these grown men, what a scene that must have been.

We asked them why they were at our school and what did they do, and how old they were? You know, all the serious but flirty questions. I mean, we really wanted to know, but we also wanted to flirt. I guess they picked up on us flirting with them and asked us to come down to the recruiting station. They were going to maximize on their charm to the fullest. I pumped the brakes just a little bit because I hadn't considered going anywhere near the Army. My homegirl was convinced that she was signing up. I was like, "Girl, what are you talking about? You don't even like doing P.E., how are you going to join the Army?" While still juniors, she complained about walking around the basketball court.

The visit to the recruiter's office turned into us making an appointment to take the Armed Services Vocational Aptitude Battery test or ASVAB. I didn't really take the test seriously, because again, I was only there for my homegirl. But a small thought in the back of my mind had me thinking that maybe, just maybe, I could do this whole Army thing.

After the test, I realized I, impressively enough, scored pretty well. Good enough that if I chose to join the Army, I could pick an administrative job. Still, I was very reluctant. After all, I was scary and probably wouldn't amount to much in the Army, at least according to my mom. I kept all my thoughts recorded in my journal and pondered.

Going to the recruiting station became a regular thing for my friend, me, and a few other kids from school. The recruiters told us to come check out this fitness program they conducted twice a week. The program was created to give future recruits a glimpse of what fitness training looked like in the Army. Every trip, my friend complained about it being too hot or she was too tired to keep going and I always asked how in the world was she going to make it in the Army!

The more I went, the more something kindled within me. I thought to myself more and more that I might just have a shot at this. I was naturally physically fit and strong, being that I was still somewhat of a tomboy and had a history of fighting boys but what put a final stamp on my interest was one day my recruiter called me over to his desk. He said he saw real potential in me. Now I'm not sure if that was legit or if that was what he had to say to meet his quota, but it was working. The last time someone told me they saw potential in me was my 6th grade teacher. I was slacking big time in his class due to all my insecurities and personal hell at home. My mom wasn't the best at academics so when we had homework to take home and I didn't understand it, I knew not to ask my mom. I already knew she wouldn't be able to help me. School work, I was good in. I answered all questions, did all my work, and read very well. My teacher called me to his desk and scolded me for not putting my brain to work in his class and sent a parent/teacher conference note home to my mom. At the meeting, he told her (which as I stated earlier he was her teacher) that I had great potential to do and be anything I wanted to be, but I had to learn to apply myself. I never forgot those words and here it was, years later, I was sitting at my recruiter's desk with him telling me the same thing.

As I came to from my thoughts, he showed me a plan of how my progression in the Army would work and all its incentives and bonuses. Each one looked appealing to me. That was my ticket out of Ocala, out of Florida. I was joining the Army.

That evening when I got in from my fitness session at the recruiting station, I presented my mom with some paperwork. I told her that I wanted to join the Army and my recruiter wanted to meet with she and I to go over the paperwork. She was still convinced that I wasn't going anywhere. My sisters and brother heard me talking about the Army and asked a bunch of questions. The main thing they wanted to know is if I was going to leave them forever. At the time, I wasn't sure so I couldn't answer. I told them that no matter what, I would be there for them.

A couple of nights later, the recruiter came over and sat with my mom and me. Her male friend was also over there (the one I said made suggestive comments at me, yeah him). He, too, didn't believe it. As the recruiter explained everything to her, she kept glancing over at me to get my reaction. I sat straight faced, but on the inside, I was jumping up and down for joy. I must admit, though, I was also a bit torn. Leaving my sisters and brother for however long hurt. I was their protector. I was their covering, but I knew in my heart, if I didn't get out of Ocala fast, I would go nowhere, fast.

After my recruiter explained everything, he presented another stack of paperwork. These were the documents that signed me over to the government. Since I was only seventeen years old, my mom would need to sign me over. She sat for what seemed like an hour, just staring from the paper to me to my recruiter. She kept asking if I was serious about this. My answer was the same each time. She even tried using scare tactics like, "You know you go to war!" I reassured her the war was long over and there wouldn't be others (okay, I know, I know...I was very naive to think that) but I was willing to say whatever I could to get those signatures on those documents. I was literally signatures away from being set free. Reluctantly, my mom signed the papers.

My recruiter gathered all documents, we all stood up and shook hands. The job was done. I belonged to Uncle Sam. He congratulated me in my living room, in front of my mom, her friend, my sisters and brother, and welcomed me into the United States Army.

Fall came fast that year, however, I anticipated it. My recruiter set my appointment to be sworn in. It was in October 1998 in Jacksonville, Florida. Dressed in my favorite tan top and plaid tan skort, I was ready to go, honey! I had my backpack packed since I would be gone for two days. All the recruits had to be at the recruiting station early, so my mom dropped me off. She left my middle sister in charge to watch the other two.

On the way to the station, my mom barely said anything to me. The tension was as thick as fog as she pulled up to the station. As I got out and said bye, she barely mumbled and drove off. At that moment, it didn't matter. I had another focus.

We all piled into a van and made the 2-hour trip up to Jacksonville. I didn't know any of the other kids on the van except my homegirl, who almost got left. I was so relieved to see her and we giggled and clowned as she got on.

It seemed like forever, but as we all woke up from our slumber, we saw where we were. We pulled up to the Military Entrance Processing Station or MEPS. As we stepped out of the van, we were greeted by other soldiers in uniform. They gave us instructions on where to go and details for our hotel rooms. Since my friend and I enlisted in the Army under the "buddy program" she and I were paired together in everything. We shared a room with two other girls who seemed pretty cool.

The two days were long and draining. They were filled with more testing, meetings, choosing our jobs and physicals. We moved from station to station. Finally, swearing in day came. We were instructed to go into one room together and wait. As we filed in, I realized some of the kids who came with us weren't in the room. I later learned, for reasons unknown to me, they weren't eligible to join.

A male soldier stood in front of us talking, I quickly glanced over to my friend. I wanted to see if she looked as nervous as I felt. Suddenly, thoughts of panic crossed my mind. "What if I can't do this?" "What if ma was right, that I am too stupid to do anything?" "Maybe I should just call to go home and just be normal again." "I'll work at the courthouse forever." I felt myself starting to sweat. Even as those thoughts crossed my mind and weighed on me heavily, I fought through them. I was not leaving. I couldn't. My life depended on it. I thought back to my many tearful conversations and daydreams up in that dogwood tree. I knew my life was more than being beat daily, belittled and degraded by my mom. My life was more than being neglected and abandoned by my father. My life was more than being used by boys for their pleasure. My life was more than what poverty had presented. So, no I wasn't leaving. I felt my feet sink deeper in place as the soldier gave us instructions to repeat after him.

"I, Lucrecia S. Q. Coleman, do solemnly affirm that I will support and defend..." I said with my right hand raised, shaky and sweaty. That was it. It was official. I was in the Army. I had to enter the delayed entry program since I was still in high school. My last step was to take an official government photo for my delayed entry card and be assigned a date to leave for basic training. I grinned so hard on that card. I was so happy, y'all. That was the first day of the rest of my life.

It's so funny how we believe one decision will be the cure all to every bad thing that's taken place in our lives. I believe that's what the Samaritan woman thought when she chose to marry five times. I believe she thought she had a chance with each man she married until the

#coffeemoments
Only, the decision never takes away the problem but invites others in to come and have a seat.

marriage ended. Instead of confronting her insecurities and facing her brokenness and dysfunction, she chose to cover it up with yet another relationship.

I wonder how many times we've done that, sisters. How many times have we made a decision, thinking it would be the one to take away all our problems?

10

On My Own

"It is our light, not our darkness that most frightens us."
---Marianne Williamson

I doubt the Samaritan woman knew the potential that rested in her broken life. There she stood, at the well, speaking with the Light of the World, Jesus Christ, and she didn't have a clue. All she saw was the shadows that had been casted over her life. And while she remained oblivious to the treasure that rested in her life, Jesus would make it all plain for her.

It didn't take long for word to get out that I had joined the Army. Along with adjusting to the new home we moved into, my mom was still a bit shocked by my decision and my middle sister and brother were upset. My youngest sister wasn't quite aware of what was going on yet. My homegirl and I were excited. We had our dates to leave, two weeks after graduating high school.

I commemorated the occasion by getting my first tattoo when I turned eighteen. Before I joined the Army, I asked my mom if I could get a tattoo. Something about ink I guess. She knew I was deathly afraid of needles so never in a million years did she expect I'd follow through with it, so she half-heartedly said yes, I could get one when I turned eighteen. And I got one. Since we never celebrated birthdays or received anything special, that was the only thing I wanted. And since I had a job and was about to graduate, I paid for my own ink. Yet again, my mom was shocked that I had followed through with something else.

I took my middle sister and one of my friends with me to a well-known tattoo shop. I had drawn up a sketch of what I wanted and handed it to the artist. He thought it was cool and went to work. I sat watching as he worked his skills onto my right calf. It was the first of several tattoos I would get. One of my goals down, one more to go. Prom.

Prom season came around quickly. I was asked out to prom by a boy who liked me. I turned him down because I figured a part of the reason he even asked me was because of the presumption that I was "easy." In my head, I wasn't easy because I did what I wanted on my terms. Besides, there was something about the idea of being free and not tied down that I wanted to experience.

My Godmother and her sister chipped in to buy my prom dress and rental car. A forest green, drop-top Chrysler Sebring. You couldn't tell me nothing! Since I had a job, I got my own hair and nails done. Slayage from head to toe. Some other girls decided that they, too, were going solo to prom, so we all cliqued up.

That night was magical! The prom was held at a beautiful outside venue, Silver Springs State Park. Soft white lights highlighted the flowers and blooms and the sweet aroma filled the air. The music was hot. "Can I Get A…" by Jay-Z featuring Amil and Ja Rule thumped over the speakers, followed by Tyrese's smooth melody "Sweet Lady."

Everyone was on the dancefloor. The football team formed their line and did their special dance moves. Everywhere I looked, something was taking place, couples taking pictures, girls in line checking their makeup and hair as they waited to get their pictures taken, boys trying to "mack" (that's that ol'school slang). There wasn't a dull moment.

As the night ended, I ran into my ex-boyfriend. The one who I gave myself to. He complimented me and asked what was I doing after the prom. Knowing good and dog on well, I had to carry my butt home, I made up some lie. I didn't want to look boring or wack in front of him and I wanted to know why he wanted to know. He asked if we could hang out. I tried (not hard enough) to give him a hard time. Didn't work. Hanging out turned into us sleeping together that night. What had I just done and why was all that crossed my mind as I looked out of my room window as he left. My mom was gone and my sisters and brother were in their rooms. They were completely unaware that I had let my ex into the house.

For some reason, I felt like filthy rags. Even though I gave myself away to other guys, this one didn't feel right. I felt used. I felt low. After all, he was the object of my savage behavior. He was the reason why I became the girl I was. Because he broke my heart. He robbed me. But even while I felt this way, because I had grown accustomed to pushing and suppressing feelings, I pushed these feelings down real deep and tried to carry on with my life.

I wonder if the way the Samaritan woman dealt with the mess of her life was to also push and suppress. It seems that that method of coping, though very unhealthy and sometimes dangerous, is a way that many of us choose to deal with our emotions or those things that need to be up front and center of our attention. Instead of creating a healthy life by facing, owning, and dealing with our issues, we create lives that are full of facades, junk, and toxic mess that eventually consumes and destroys us.

#coffeemoments
I didn't realize every time I gave myself away to someone, I chipped away a bit of my soul and handed it to them on a platter.

Not long after prom, guys I never suspected, approached me, asking for sex. Wait, what? Though very surprised and slightly insulted by these propositions, there was a small, well maybe moderately big part of me that was entertained by them. Guys wanted me. Guys paid attention to me. And again, I gave in. I didn't realize that every time I connected myself with another soul, we became one, creating a soul tie. 1 Corinthians 6:16 (The Message) "There's more to sex than mere skin on skin. Sex is as much spiritual mystery as physical fact. As written in Scripture, "The two become one." Since we want to become spiritually one with the Master, we must not pursue the kind of sex that *avoids commitment and intimacy, leaving us lonelier than ever...*" (emphasis added).

I went from savage to reckless quick. My mentality was focused on the attention I received. It was focused on getting rid of the labels of abandonment, rejection, and neglect. It was focused on filling the gaping holes in my soul. And I thought sleeping with guys would filled those holes. I didn't realize my behavior only made the holes bigger and deeper.

I was ready to leave. I was ready to leave Ocala behind and all the drama that came along with it. My relationship with my mom was broken. She had yet again gotten married (#4) and again became consumed with her new husband. I felt myself wrestling with respecting her and her treatment towards me didn't make it easier.

Though I enjoyed working at the courthouse, I knew my time was winding down. I had already told my boss when my last day at the office would be so they threw me a going away party. It was the warmest thing to feel accepted. My supervisor cried like I was her child. I reassured her that I would be back by to see her (which I kept my word and did go back to see her).

Graduation day finally came. I didn't graduate with honors, barely a decent GPA, but nonetheless, I was done. In only two more weeks, I'd be off to a new chapter in my life.

The last class of the millennium (1999) walked the stage. The feeling was incredible. As I took my diploma and shook everyone's hands, I threw my arms up in the air, a symbol of victory.

Waiting to leave seemed like an eternity. I got involved in a *"situationship"* with an older man. He was well known around town and was a drug dealer. He frequently picked me up from home while my mom was away at work and we'd joy ride all over the town. While I was living it up with my new situation, what I didn't know was he had warrants for his arrest, carried drugs and weapons in his car. And here I was driving his car around town like I owned it. All I can say is, But God and His saving grace. Since I knew nothing further would come out of my messing around with the drug dealer, I didn't feel any type of way when we suddenly parted ways.

My mom, my sisters, and brother drove me to the recruiting station. It was early morning on June 17, 1999 as we pulled up. Several other recruits were also pulling in. The time was here, the time to start my new life had come. Through my excitement, I fought to look at the pained faces of my siblings. I knew what they faced when I left and my heart hurt for them. Although my sister and I fought like wild animals, I felt solely responsible for the safety and well-being of my siblings. I especially felt bad for my brother. I was the only one who understood him. I almost felt as if I was abandoning them. But as I stood watching the tears stream from their faces, I knew in my heart I was making the right decision. I knew my time in Ocala had come to an end when I first set eyes on the recruiters at my high school. I had to go.

My mom, to my surprise, was also emotional. She hugged me and said she would miss me. This was harder than I imagined. My brother sat silently in the back seat. His face was wet with tears but his forehead in a hard frown. I tried explaining again that I'd be back for them, but one of the recruiters interrupted me with his announcement to load up on the van. I had to say my goodbyes quickly.

I got on the van, scared out of my mind, but crazy excited for what was to come. As I settled into the seat, I quickly looked around to see if my homegirl was already seated. She wasn't. "Where is this girl?" I thought as I panicked a bit. I didn't want to do this alone. Besides, I was sitting on this van because of her bright idea for us to join. Little did I know and would later learn many, many years later, that God only used her as conduit to draw me into my destiny. I wonder, in your own lives, Because if you look back over your life hard enough, you would probably be able to pinpoint that instance that was lifechanging. Sometimes those instances aren't pretty. Rather, they are a hot mess, but nonetheless, God in His Sovereign ability, can take even the worst and ugliest of situations and still cause it to work out for your good (Romans 8:28). That's exactly what He did for me.

#coffeemoments

How many conduits has God used to get to you?

How many situations, experiences, relationships has God used to push us towards our destiny?

h

I woke up to an abrupt halt of the van. We were parked on the premises of Fort Jackson, South Carolina. Seconds later came loud, terrifying yelling. It didn't take long before I saw where the yelling was coming from. Two very large, scary looking men with strange looking hats on walked quickly through the van yelling at everyone on board. "Get off the freaking vehicle, RIGHT NOW!" "You're on my turf now!" "Move! Move! MOVE!" The bulging veins from the foreheads and necks had me in awe. I was deathly terrified! "What did I get myself into?" I thought as I frantically scurried out of the van. "Line up! Line up, RIGHT NOW!" came more screaming. There were about ten of us standing shoulder to shoulder outside of the van.

The smell of the earth waking up hit my nose as more of those men came running out. They charged us like rabid dogs on the loose. I wanted to cry so badly, but held it in because I saw where that got one of the other girls in the line. The hat one guy wore was knocking her in the forehead as he barked at her, which made her crying intensify. *"Please just stop crying!"* I begged her in my mind. I felt so sorry for her and sorry for us.

While she was being chewed to pieces, 3 females came charging at us. Their hats looked different from the ones the men wore, but their demeanor was just as terrifying. "You thought you were cute then, but your (expletive) belong to me now!" "You ain't got your mama here to take up for you now!" "What you looking at? You got something to say?" one of the women said as she stared down a girl standing right next to me. It felt like we had been standing out in the dark for an eternity getting eaten alive by cannibals. The girl quietly sucked her teeth. I held my breath because I wanted to make sure the female soldier knew that sound did NOT come from me. The woman with the hat ran over with lightning speed and cursed that girl straight out. This was what I had gotten myself into and my homegirl was nowhere in sight.

I finally saw her a few weeks later. I was so glad to see a familiar face but my excitement quickly fizzled out as I got closer to her. Her foot was casted and she hobbled over to me on crutches. Looking incredibly puzzled, I asked, "Girl, what happened to you?" She said she "sprang" her ankle and was going home. WHAT?! Going home! "WHAT? How when we signed up TOGETHER! I'm here because of YOU and you're LEAVING ME?!" I screamed. I couldn't believe what I was hearing. I was being abandoned, again, by someone I thought cared for me. I had been hoodwinked and bamboozled. She apologized, barely looking at my face. She slowly turned and hobbled away. Just like that. I was left alone, again and that would be the last time I'd ever see her again.

Training was difficult. I had never been challenged like this before in my life and I was doing it all alone. Drill sergeants rode us day in and day out. Yelling, spitting, cursing, and smoking us was what much of the days consisted of. *(Side note: smoking consisted of long, grueling exercises repeated over and over in a rigorous manner).*

Every day was another obstacle to climb over. For 9 weeks, we endured around the clock work outs, sleepless nights, outside field exercises, exhausting road marches, death by power point slides, etc. We were tempted daily during lunch time with mouth-watering desserts. The drill sergeants lurked around waiting for one of us to slip up and eat something. And it happened.

You would've thought that since nobody else ate a dessert, that this one guy would follow suit. Wrong! He helped himself to not one, but TWO slices of cake. Where was his battle buddy? All the drill sergeants around sat looking and laughing. They knew what was up and so did we. As we shoveled the food down our throats, we glared angrily at the guy who chose to indulge himself. The other guys had special plans for him later that night. It wasn't until his last bite that he realized what he had done. Too late.

Our feet didn't hit the ground good when the drill sergeants started barking out commands for us to drop and push. We were so full from having just eaten (and skipping meals wasn't an option). For what seemed like forever, we got smoked (tortured). The male drill sergeant got in the face of the guy who ate the cakes and blamed all of this on him. People began vomiting as the third round of the smoke session came. I don't know if I've ever prayed as hard as I did in my head. If I cried it wasn't noticeable because of the large beads of sweat that fell from my face. So, I cried.

h

Graduation day from basic training finally came. My class A uniform fit perfectly around my petite, muscular frame. Basic training did many things to me and one was it most definitely did my body good. It was time to walk across the field and graduate. My feet ached from the long road march we had just completed the night before. Blisters rubbed hard against my dress shoes, but I was determined to march so I sucked the pain up. My family sat in the bleachers ready to see me walk. My mom, along with her new husband, my sisters, brother, and new step brothers sat eagerly waiting.

The music cued and we marched. We stood in the South Carolina heat for fort-five minutes in our class A's, which consisted of a wool jacket, wool pants, short sleeve cotton shirt, black dress socks, black shoes, and a garrison cap. I was drenched. Everything I wore was ringing wet. We were warned repeatedly to wiggle our toes and not to lock our knees or we would pass out. I guess some people had forgotten because they dropped like flies. Another prayer meeting was going on in my head as my legs quivered. I felt light headed. I felt my legs giving out. Before I lost my footing, the ceremony was over. It was done. We were officially graduates of basic training.

The oddest thing happened after the ceremony. While we should have been running to greet our family and friends and get the heck out of there, we all stood around the drill sergeants waiting for them to give us our next order. We had gotten so used to being told what to do. We had a male and female drill sergeant and they both stood talking to us. They shared how we were their best and most challenging class. The male drill teared up as he let us go. Even though those were some of the most grueling 9 weeks of my life, I knew I would never forget the lessons.

I ran over to my family and hugged them all. I was actually very happy to see familiar faces again. I introduced my new friends to my family and we exchanged addresses (since you know, cell phones were still somewhat new). My visit with my family was short-lived because immediately following graduation, we had to prepare to move into phase two of the Army

Before I headed to basic training, I got to pick out my occupation at MEPS. Because I had pretty good scores, I chose a military pay technician. The next leg of my enlistment was to transfer to a different part of Fort Jackson and complete training known as Advanced Individual Training or AIT. Training for this occupation lasted for 8 weeks and was very intense. We would essentially be responsible for maintaining the pay accounts of every servicemember in the military worldwide. I fell in love. I absolutely loved training for my job.

Comparing AIT to basic training was like day and night. We had a bit more freedom and privileges. We got to go around post and off post once we moved through phases. The drill sergeants were still crazy but also cool. We eventually learned to accept and sometimes look beyond their crazy.

I met some of the coolest people ever in AIT. Honestly, it felt like I was in college, even though I didn't know what going to college felt like. So many of us were just graduating high school and this was our first time on our own. We got the opportunity to grow and experience adulthood together.

Our privileges came in three phases. It was in the last phase where I got my first taste of alcohol and club life. We were given permission to have a one night, overnight. That meant we got to stay outside of the post for a night. Some people opted to either go to their home or relatives' homes if they lived in the area. Others, myself included, chose to stay the night at a hotel.

I was nervous out of my mind. The closest I had been to a club was at the YMCA back home when they would throw events for the teenagers. I always used to hear kids talking about hanging out at the golf course back in Ocala but I was never allowed to go. Though I was nervous, I couldn't show it. I was with about six other people and they all were ready to get on with the night.

Since all of us were under age, we found a random guy at the gas station who agreed to get us alcohol (he knew he was wrong and so were we). We all waited in the cab as he brought our purchases back to the taxi. One of the guys paid him twenty dollars for doing the favor. Oh, my goodness, as I'm writing this, I am cracking up because I'm reliving the moment and shaking my head. We were terribly naïve back then.

One of the girls yanked open the bags and we all marveled at all the alcohol inside. Absolut and Bacardi Lemon were two of the bottles. The taxi driver took us back to the hotel and we all popped bottles and decided we wanted to go out.

We ended up at some little club but I don't think any of us cared; we were just happy to be out. The music was loud and popping, smoke blew everywhere, and small groups of people clustered all around. I decided to taste the Absolut first. My throat burned as I drank it. I guess the face I made caused everybody to laugh at me. By the end of the night, the burning sensation was gone and I was floating on clouds.

I don't remember walking back to the hotel room or hooking up with one of the guys we came with. Everything was a blur, but my friends made it apparent to me that something had happened. "Girl you had some fun last night, huh?" one of the girls called out to me. She sat on the bed looking at me sideways with a smirk on her face. I replied that I didn't know what she was talking about but deep down knew that something had happened between me and one of the guys who was with us.

Before leaving the hotel room, I took a glimpse in the mirror to straighten out my newly cut hair. As I combed it out, I looked down at my neck and noticed a huge dark mark. "Oh crap!" I thought to myself. A hickey. A ginormous hickey.

I remember the last time I had those on my body, my mom nearly tore my skin off. I was still in high school and was being fresh and met this boy out on the softball field of a school one night. I let him suck away at my neck, leaving golf ball sized hickies. My necked itched and ached so bad but I felt cool because hickies were a sign of "getting it on." And even though I didn't necessarily want to display my marks, I wanted to fit in.

Since I had long micro braids, I tried hard covering my marks up when I got back home. My mom looked at me suspiciously and riddled me with questions. My middle sister had her suspicions too and came into the kitchen to get in on the action. She knew something was going down. At first, I tried coming up with every lie in the book as to why I was acting weird and why my neck was super stiff. The last lie was that I had gotten stung by a huge bee and it was causing my neck to swell and stiffen. I am the worst liar in the world y'all. I may get the lie out but my face and mannerisms tell on me with the quickness.

I knew the lie had hit a brick wall. Then my mom snatched my hair from around my neck. A deep gasp was all I heard before a loud smack across my face. I felt fire and saw stars. My mom slapped the color off my cheek. I knew I was dead. I was a senior in high school and just knew I wasn't going to make it out alive.

That same feeling came over me all over again as I stood in the mirror, looking in disbelief at the huge mark on my neck. I scanned the room to see if anybody else noticed my neck but they were all in their own world.

The suspected guy I had my way with looked over at me and gave a slight head nod and smirk. Great! I barely knew the dude and gave myself to him. I told myself that I wasn't going to go down that road anymore since leaving home. Being in basic training helped take away the urges to have sex, but I continued masturbating. I thought I had a grip on this sex thing

#coffeemoments
But as long as the root remains intact and lies dormant, it will rest until the right stimulant or trigger comes along and rekindles it all over again.

but realized I didn't after all.

I wonder how many of us make the vain attempt to put a cap on a bad habit. We figuratively wrap it up in chains, toss it over the bridge, and stand dusting our hands off as if to say, "good riddance." What we don't realize, however, is that thing we try so badly to escape from, never goes anywhere. We may have learned to suppress the symptom or chop off the stem.

11

What is a Woman's Worth?

"Dirty diamonds are still diamonds."
---Dr. Tony Evans

The woman at the well had a bad reputation. She wasn't seen for more than just a woman who couldn't get her life together. Who would want to listen to anything she had to say? She was jacked up! Unfortunately, the community around her saw and labeled her as dirty and unfit. But Jesus saw her as a diamond in the ruff, an opportunity for greatness and everlasting beauty. And He used her and gifted her life with a testimony that would transform generations.

I woke up from my nap at my mom's husband's house. I had since graduated AIT and was now awaiting my departure to Europe. I had a week to go before I left and I absolutely could NOT wait. Being back in Ocala put a stale taste in my mouth and seeing people doing the same things they had done before I left, made the taste even more stale.

Staying in the house of another man was foreign and uncomfortable to me. It's not like I didn't know my mom's husband, I just didn't like the idea of having to share space with another man, only this time, he called the shots. He tried making my short stay as comfortable as he could, but it didn't work. Previous experiences from other men in my life had shot that right down.

I kept a low profile and didn't want to be bothered by anyone. I even felt distant from my own family. My mom returned to her old ways and made slick comments at me, attempting to make me crumble. I guess it was the constant mental and physical beatdowns I got in basic training that toughened me up a bit because I didn't as much as flinch at her comments. My siblings wanted badly to come with me to Europe and I told them I would get them as soon as I got settled over there. I imagined the beautiful life I'd have with my siblings over there.

I was going to Germany, to be exact. What an amazing experience we all would have there! I mean, we were four poor, traumatized kids from the hood who could only dream of a place like Germany. And here it was, I was the ticket to their freedom. I relished the thought.

My time to leave for Europe had finally arrived. My mom drove me to Gainesville International Airport. This was my first time on an airplane and I was the first in my immediate family to fly. My nerves were done thinking of flying over the Atlantic Ocean, but at the same time I was super excited.

Of course, my siblings were very sad so I reassured them as best as I could that I would send for them. As I finished up my goodbyes, the announcer came over the intercom inviting passengers to board the plane. My eyes filled with tears and blurred my vision as I got in line to leave. I handed my boarding pass to the clerk and walked through the passageway that forever changed my life.

Nothing worked to calm my nerves as the plane took off. Seeing us take off and into the air was surreal. I sat in a window seat and absolutely refused to look out of the window, at first anyway. Fortunately, I was seated next to a very nice woman. She must've saw me struggling in my seat and she grabbed my hand. She reassured me that it would be alright and for me to try to relax as much as possible. Being that the flight was nine hours, it would be in my best interest to calm down or my flight would be long and torturous.

The plane leveled and settled at a comfortable altitude. Though I was scared out of my mind, I mustered up some nerves and took a quick peek out the window. It was a resplendent site! Never in my life had I witnessed the stars as close as I did that night. As we traveled through time zones, I could see the dark earth below. We had long crossed over land, which twinkled with the lights of human activity and was now flying over the Atlantic Ocean. It was pitch black. Fluffy, white clouds whisked by as they gave way to a clear, star speckled sky. I couldn't take my eyes off the site.

As I write this, my mind drifted back to the day my life changed.

The food served on the airplane was amazing. There's two places I've learned that has the best food: airplanes and hospitals. Can I get an amen?

I finished up my ginger ale (now a staple drink) and decided to try and catch a nap. I removed my chunky, grey boots and threw a blanket over me. The nice lady who calmed my nerves, was resting next to me and I just laid my head on her shoulder. I still chuckle about that to this day.

#coffeemoments
Up until that point of being on the plane, I didn't think I was good for anything or that I would amount to anything. After all, that's what I had heard my entire life. And there it was, I sat on a flight to Europe. That moment was impactful.

I guess I was in a good sleep because the announcement that we were landing, startled me awake. I scrambled trying to put my shoes back on my feet but couldn't. I looked down and noticed my feet looked like sausages. I guess the compression of the plane caused my feet to swell up when I took my boots off. Great! I wasn't going to let swollen feet stop me from strutting in those boots. They were brand new boots I'd bought specifically for that trip.

Outside was gloomy and grey. Different from what I'd left back in the states. Without being outside, I could tell it was freezing. After all, it was the beginning of December and I'd heard the stories of how cold it could get in Europe. I so was not prepared.

I clucked and clicked my way through the airport. My feet felt like stuff pigs in a blanket but I kept it moving. I had on my five-inch grey ankle boots, matching skin tight skinny jeans, a black top with a cut out in the chest, and a small black leather jacket. You couldn't tell me nothing! As I walked towards the baggage claim, or what I thought was the baggage claim area, I looked around the airport.

I felt like I was in another world. The language sounded like gibberish. Dogs walked about freely with their owners. The air smelled weird. There were signs for everything and they all looked weird. Rhein Main airport was bustling with bodies. Among those bodies, stood the person on detail to pick me up to transport me to my unit, my new squad leader.

He picked me up and drove back to Mannheim. Darkness had fallen fast as well as the temperature. I so wasn't prepared for this arctic weather. We grabbed a quick bite to eat and went on to where I'd be staying. I was taken to an old three-story building that looked haunted. I'm pretty sure if I could recount, I'll remember seeing and hearing stuff I shouldn't have heard. Since I was fresh off the plane, I was given some Vietnam Army green linens to hold me over until I could buy my own. Yuck! Those things itched terribly in basic training and AIT and here I was, stuck with them again.

I was given a quick tour of the barracks and was pointed to the nearest telephone; a paid phone on the third floor, the male floor. Still dressed in my grey and black outfit, I dropped my bags off in my room and made my way up to the third floor. I clucked and clacked down the hall, apparently getting the attention of the males who lived on that floor. I made my way to the telephone and called my mother. I guess the guys could tell I was a newbie because they lingered out in the hallway. Here we go!

I told my mom about my ventures thus far and told her to tell my sisters and brother I made it and I loved them. After hanging up with my mom, I turned to leave but was greeted by one of the guys who lived on that floor. Immediately, I got a bad vibe from him. He riddled me with questions but I barely answered. I zig zagged around him and made my way back downstairs. I guess he thought I was playing hard to get because he continued, almost daily, bothering me.

A month passed and I had settled into my new home for the next couple of years. I learned my way around town, thanks to my new friends. It was mandatory that we take language and culture classes so I knew some Deutsch, at least enough to order food, cause ya girl had to eat.

One of my homegirls kept watch over me. She was eight years older than me and took on the role of "mama/homegirl" since I was only 19 years old. Though I laughed at her calling herself scolding me, it comforted me to know she had my back. Then I learned what PCS was.

Permanent change of station or PCS was what happened regularly in the military. A service member would serve out his or her time in a designated area and then they'd be assigned to another location. That's what happened to my homegirl. She was heading back to the states. I was a bit shaken up because I felt like I was being left alone. I learned quickly that was the way of the military.

Luckily, my loneliness didn't last long. I met another girl who loved to party. Her and I hit the club every weekend; which our weekend started on a Thursday, by the way. One of our regular spots was a hole in the wall called The Top Hat or "The Hat." Banging music, delicious drinks, and a wild crowd filled the atmosphere every Friday night. My friend and I stepped out looking fresh, ready to dance and drink the night away. I guess I left my guard back at my room because one particular night changed into something unexpected really quick.

My girl and I were on the dancefloor, drinks in hand, popping and rolling. We hated being restricted and dancing with guys so we always opted to dance with each other. Juvenile's "Back That Thang Up" (clean title) had just gone off and we made our way to the bar for more drinks. The days of paying for a drink were long over when we learned how to use what we had to get what we wanted. The bar tender asked me to blow him some kisses and drinks were on him. Of course, I did just that and gave a little dance for "GP." My homegirl did the same. The bar tender smiled, winked, and mixed together our favorite drinks.

As we sat, chatting, recharging, and looking over the crowd, the guy from the barracks came over towards me. I immediately turned my face into a grimace and turned back around to face the bar. He sat next to me and tried to hold a conversation. Again, that same creepy feeling I got when I first met him came right back. I asked him to leave me be and to go mess with some other chick. Yet, he still didn't take no for an answer. So instead of me further entertaining him, I turned to my girlfriend and ignored him. Bad move on my part.

I turned back around for my drink and finished it off so I could dance some more. I had gotten drunk before but this type of drunk hit me hard and quick. I felt **really** drunk. I made my way to the dance floor with my homegirl but everything started swaying back and forth. She asked was I okay and I said yeah. A dude she had been wanting to hook up with (yeah in that way) came behind her. She instantly started grinding on him.

While I looked on at her getting freaky, I felt a hand go around my waist. I turned to see it was the guy from the barracks. He was trying to dance with me. I tried pushing him off me but with no luck at all. I felt very weak, sluggish, and dizzy. The guy wrapped his arm around me as if to help me walk. It became harder for me to fight him off. I guess it didn't look obvious that I didn't want to go with him because half of us in there were drunk and trying to get hooked up for the night. He lead me to a cab outside the club and guided me in.

I think I blacked out because when I woke up, it was the next morning and I was in somebody else's room. My head was spinning and I felt like I was going to vomit. I looked down at my naked body lying in a bed in a tumble of sheets. Still dazed and confused, I noticed the sheets moving. From in between my legs, the dude raised his head. I attempted to utter something, but blacked out again.

I don't know how long I stayed out but I woke up to water running in the bathroom. When I got my focus, I saw the guy come walking out of the bathroom with a towel wrapped around his waist. He stood in the doorway and nonchalantly looked at me for a second then proceeded to brush his hair in the mirror.

Without uttering a word, I slipped my naked body out of the bed and rushed to put my clothes on. My body ached with pain as I walked quickly out of the room. I felt like I was walking down the hall of shame. Guys walked in and out of their rooms, some surprised to see me exit out of the guy's room. One of his home boys called out to me but I kept walking. My short hair was messy and my clothes smelled like last night's smoke. I ran into my room and hopped into the shower. I had just been violated but no one would know, until now, eighteen years later.

Time went by and my drinking, partying, and sex life got worse. I maintained good behavior professionally but behind closed doors, I was on a rampage. I had sex with just about anyone I set my eyes on and who suited the bill for me. I drank myself numb to get through what my flesh craved. I started using guys for their time, pleasure, and money. I had established another marker in my mind, that another guy would never violate me ever again. My worth became rooted in what I could get with my body. My value had been sized down to what men were willing to pay.

I have a strong feeling that many of us perpetrate. We fake the funk in portraying to be this independent, well put together woman who knows her worth. We front like we're calling the shots. Truth be told, our bad decisions call the shots. How we treat ourselves or the lack thereof, determines how other people will treat us. The woman at the well sat in the same seat many of us has at one time sat in or may still be sitting in. She went through marriage five times and still didn't understand. The "situationship" Jesus found her in was one dictated by her lack of understanding what her worth was.

#coffeemoments
We move blindly through relationships, situationships, friends with benefitships, and all other types of ships because we are ignorant to the worth God established on our lives.

And that's how several of us live out our lives.

But just like the encounter the woman at the well had with Jesus, we can have that same one. Just have to be willing.

12

Oh, Baby!

"Be the kind of woman you want your daughter to be."
—Lucrecia Slater

The bible doesn't state if the woman at the well had any children. However, I just can't help but to wonder if she thought she would be a good example to her children. I wonder if she counted herself out of the role of being that example for any children she may have had. Just as Jesus took her broken life and redeemed it, He can and will do the same for you and me.

I moved blindly through situation after situation, not realizing the damage I was doing to myself. I didn't understand that what I carried from my childhood, how I thought about myself, and how I allowed myself to be treated, all aided in my spiritual death. And along the way, I brought several people with me.

#coffeemoments
I didn't realize how much bigger I was making the holes in my broken soul.

You know what's funny? Amid me figuratively killing myself, God brought someone along my path to warn me. He was a bible thumping, fast talking, hyper man. He worked a few offices down from me. He was married with two adorable daughters. John always carried a tattered looking suitcase wherever he went and inside was a tattered bible. He was a Specialist (E4) and back then, when the Army was the real Army (yep I said it) we had to show respect to Specialists. I don't think many people took John seriously though.

One day, he busted into the office I worked in and bee-lined straight towards my desk. I saw him coming but continued working and bumping "Thong Song" by Sisqo on my computer. I was psyching myself out for the club that night.

John came over and dropped his dusty suitcase on my desk. He popped it open and pulled out that tattered bible. He asked me a question that would stick with me for the rest of my life. "If Jesus came back right now, where would you go, heaven or hell?" I paused my song and looked at him with a look that could kill. Not only had he interrupted my vibe, but he had the nerve to ask me some mess like that? I hadn't thought about God since I was a little girl. I mean, I still believed in Him but He was no longer a part of my life anymore. I was "grown" and was in charge of my own life. "I guess heaven, I don't know! Why you even asked me that?" I asked as I sucked my teeth. I suppose he knew my answer because he didn't waste time flipping to a scripture that would also forever be with me. "Read this!" John said as he shoved the bible at me. Looking down at what he pointed to, I began to read. *"I know your works, that you are neither cold nor hot. I could wish you were cold or hot. So then, because you are lukewarm, neither cold nor hot, I will vomit you out of My mouth."* (Revelation 3:15-16, New King James Version).

I didn't have a clue of what that meant but I didn't like it. Then John pretty much told me I was going to hell if I didn't straighten out my life. The nerve he had! I said okay, but not before I went to the club first. I know, I was ratchet in my thinking. But deep down inside, I knew he was right. If I didn't seek the One who had created me to straighten my life out, I was heading to hell. Unfortunately, after all I'd been through, it wasn't enough to slow me down. Yet.

John never gave up on me, even after the towel was pretty much dragging in my hand. I guess I must've still had an inkling of hope because I couldn't quite find it in me to throw in the towel completely. After about a hundred invitations to his church, I finally accepted. He was overwhelmed with joy and said he would be by the barracks in the church van to pick me up first thing Sunday morning. Great.

Now, I had nothing close to church attire in my closet. The best thing I had was a very short, two-piece white dress set. It was a dress with spaghetti straps and a small jacket to go over it. The only shoes I had at the time were my "go get em girl" shoes (for those who may not be familiar, very high heeled, platformed stilettos). I had always heard church folk say, "come as you are" so I went as I was.

Lord, if looks could cast one straight into hell, I would've been there ten times over in a split second! John's wife greeted me as I went inside the church, but others greeted me with dagger eyes, scan-overs, whispers, and turned up lips. Being that I was very much still worldly and ratchet, it would've taken nothing for me to tell them about themselves and keep it moving. But John's wife grabbed me and lead me in. She had to serve that day so she couldn't sit with me.

I can't tell you how uncomfortable I felt in that place. Many women treated me as if I had the plague and the men either gawked or were afraid to look my way. After church service was over, a middle-aged woman approached me. I saw her coming my way and had prepared her blast out in my mind. "If she says one thing sideways out of her neck, she's getting it!" I thought to myself as she sat next to me.

My face was set like stone as she greeted me. Then she said, "honey, "I am so glad you came. You look beautiful and I hope to see you again." The stone expression softened into a small, relieved smile and I thanked her and told her I would try to return. She hugged me and walked me outside.

Sisters, let me express something to you from the depths of my heart. Believe it or not, I believe we will attract many more young ladies into the church if we changed our perspective and attitude towards them. Not everyone will have a standard church outfit when they first start attending church. If we looked back at our lives, I'm sure we'll see that none of us floated on clouds in a white gown from birth. If so, sister you must have been left out of heaven. But we all have messy origins.

#coffeemoments
I understand that scripture refers to husbands and households, but check this, in order to do and be all those things, a young woman must first learn how to treat herself.

What needs to be celebrated is the fact that that young sister even came to church! It's time out for fake smiling in their faces then whispering behind their backs or casting them into hell at first glance. They need Jesus just like you and me. Love covers all. God commands us, seasoned ladies, to teach the younger generation how to live godly lives (refer to Titus 2). And that comes through us sharpening each other (Proverbs 27:17). So, don't shun her, love and cover her.

I didn't immediately return to church. The pull of partying, drinking, and having sex was stronger than my desire to go to church. Funny how circumstances can shut all of that down.

I met my daughter's father not long after my assault. He and I kicked it for about two weeks before becoming sexually active. Three months after meeting him, I became pregnant. Instantly, I panicked. I was nineteen and about to become a mother.

The morning I found out, I knew something was off. I knew my menstrual cycle was supposed to come that day but it never showed up. I had never been on any type of birth control and I played Russian Roulette with condoms, so I panicked. Honestly, at first, I thought I had contracted something. But a small thought that begged to differ lead me to the store for a pregnancy test.

Before taking the test, I sat on the toilet, heart pounding out of my chest. Thoughts ran crazily through my mind. This wasn't supposed to happen like this! I didn't even want children. I hated them and they hated me, mutual feelings. What and how was I supposed to raise a child? Besides raising my siblings, I didn't know the first thing about raising my own child.

Sparing myself further agony, I took the test. Positive. I was pregnant or at least according to the test. My boyfriend was laying in the bed when I walked out and showed him the results. He said a curse word and the next thing to come out of his mouth was, "You sure it's mine?" Y'all if I could've turned into a flea and hopped my happy behind right out of that room, I would have. I can't even tell you how low I felt in that moment.

To mask my embarrassment, I responded with a curse word and sarcastically asked who else could I be pregnant by. After a moment of awkward silence, he told me I should make an appointment at the military clinic (Troop Medical Clinic or TMC). But to do that, I had to let my supervisors know. More embarrassment. I had only been in my new unit for three months and here it was, I could be pregnant.

I sat nervously in the waiting room of the clinic, waiting for my results. After what felt like forever, the military physician came out to get me. He took me to his office and sighed as he sat down. Without him saying anything, I already knew the results. His words took me by surprise though.

"Private Coleman, I have the results from your pregnancy test and you are pregnant. Now, I know you just joined the military and you have your whole career ahead of you. There are options you could take so that this pregnancy doesn't hinder your progression." I looked at him like he was going to come back with something else. But he sat, looking at me dead in my eyes, serious as ever. He was suggesting that I have an abortion.

I replied as calmly as I could, "Sir, if you're suggesting that I get an abortion, I will certainly NOT! I did this to myself so I will have to go through the consequences. How could you even suggest this to me?" Tears welled in my eyes. I didn't have anybody familiar around me. My family were thousands of miles away and here this Captain was, telling me to get an abortion. His cheeks flushed red as he responded, "I understand how this sounds, I just figured since you are so young and again, have your whole career ahead of you, that you would consider..." Tact went out of the window. Before I even let him complete his sentence, I stood up, thanked the Captain for providing the results, and left his office. On the way out, one of the clerks handed me a slip. The slip was proof that I had been to the clinic. There was another form stapled to the back of the slip. I flipped it over to look and there it was, a pregnancy profile.

As I handed the forms to my squad leader, I felt like it all wasn't real. My boyfriend didn't seem too enthused to hear the news, considering he was already the father of a two-year old girl. Even though I had rejected everything the physician told me days before in his office, the thoughts of possibly aborting this child lingered. I thought back to my mom and how she struggled without the support of our fathers. I didn't want to be like that. I pondered the idea of aborting this child for the next few months.

By this time, my whole unit knew I was pregnant, but I still tried to hide it. I shied away from anyone asking me questions about being pregnant. People asked if I knew what I was having and what did I want to have. I brushed all questions off. I wasn't even supposed to be pregnant! I hated kids and they hated me! All of that changed when I felt the baby move for the first time.

My unit had new barracks built across the street from the old, haunted ones. They were so nice and literally a breath of fresh air. It was on a weekend and I laid across my bed watching Austin Powers for the thousandth time.

I was still contemplating aborting the child when I felt a soft nudge in my belly. I sat up and sat still, waiting to see if I was tripping, had gas, or really felt something. Because all before that moment, I hadn't felt anything and frankly didn't care to feel anything. After a few more moments, not only did I feel the nudge again, but I saw the little knob of a body part slightly poke through my belly. I gasp and tears immediately flooded my eyes. I had a life growing inside of me.

The thought hit me hard and I jumped on my cell phone and called my boyfriend. He never answered so I hung up and called again. Still no answer. I wanted someone to celebrate in this moment with me, so I grabbed my roommate. Her face filled with the biggest smile when the child in my belly kicked again. The rest of that day, I was thrilled. It had finally dawned on me that I could never and would never abort the child growing in my womb or any child after that.

I finally heard from my boyfriend a few days later. Turns out that he had gotten into a lot of trouble and was on restriction and very limited to what he could do and where he could go. Because I was still new to all the Army lingo and how things worked, I thought he was lying and just was making up excuses to stay away from me. Turns out he wasn't lying. He had indeed gotten into a lot of trouble and was now being forced to get out of the military or ETS (expiration of term of service).

He was escorted over to my room two weeks after I had last spoken to him. So of course, you know I was highly upset and feeling some kind of way. He explained that he was returning to his home state of New York. All feelings of anger flew out of the window and feelings of sadness and despair flooded me instead. "What am I supposed to do by myself?" I desperately asked. All I could see were images of my mom struggling to take care of us and almost losing her mind as a result. I didn't want to wear those same shoes. And then my boyfriend offered a suggestion.

He said the only way he could see his child was for us to get married. He said that would guarantee him to come back to Europe after getting out of the Army. That was his way of proposing, y'all. But I didn't know the truth

#coffeemoments My mind painted a picture that reality wasn't ready for.

from a can of paint at the time. All I knew was that I was no longer going to be alone. I would raise my child alongside the father. We would be a family. Immediately, my mind started filling with fantasies and a happy family and that picket fence.

Everything seemed to move so fast. My boyfriend had to leave Europe and go back to the states to apply for his passport. As time went by, my belly grew bigger. I asked one of my co-workers to take me to find out the sex of my baby. The sight was surreal. There was a little person in my womb, a little girl. She sucked her thumb and turned her backside up to the camera; I guess she demanded her privacy even in the womb. Hot tears streamed down my face as I watched the strong heart beat stream across the monitor. How could I have been so close to entertaining the thought of aborting this life within me? I thank God so much for not allowing me to act on that thought. My co-worker sat close by watching, smiling, and silently shedding tears as well. My little girl was strong and all mine. I knew in that moment that I would shower her with love. I vowed on that table looking at my baby in my womb, that everything I went through in my life, she would never be exposed to in hers. She would know from the onset that my love for her was true and ran deep. I was going to be a mommy. At nineteen, I was going to be responsible for another life.

By the time I reached six months of pregnancy, I had to prepare for the transition of moving out of the barracks and into my own apartment. I never lived on my own before so this was a big step. I was only a PFC (Private First Class), so I didn't make much money at all, although I thought I was balling before I got pregnant.

My unit threw me a huge baby shower and provided me with necessities and supplies for my baby that lasted until she grew to almost six months (after being born). Yeah, I'd say they looked out for ya girl quite well. My First Sergeant took me under his wing and figuratively adopted me as his daughter. When he first met my boyfriend, he riddled him with twenty-one questions. When he found out I was pregnant, he scolded me then nurtured me through my pregnancy. People donated furniture, kitchen supplies, bedroom supplies, and everything else I'd need to get me by in my new place. I was and still am very thankful.

Not long after I moved into my apartment, my boyfriend returned to Germany. What I had pictured in my mind, was not at all what played out. I went from being happy and having all these happy thoughts about us as a family, to being miserable and depressed. I had anxiety and panic attacks, one which landed me in the hospital with the doctors stopping my labor. I ended up returning to the hospital on several occasions, just stressed out.

My boyfriend hung around lowlifes and smoked weed. He played mind games with me and constantly threatened to return to the states. Because I clung on to the image of who I didn't want to become (my mom), I begged him to stay and said that I'd do right.

Again, I didn't have an example of what a healthy marriage or relationship for that matter, looked like. I didn't know how to value myself. I didn't understand my worth or the strength God placed inside of me. All I knew was that I was nineteen and pregnant and I didn't want to raise this child on my own. After he seemed satisfied with my begging, he chose to stay.

#coffeemoments
What I would learn several years later, is that dysfunction is a great manipulator and distorter of what and how we see things and the way we think.

There were several red flags that prompted me not to go through with marriage. But out of desperation to be normal, dismissed all flags. I wanted the dysfunction in my life to just disappear and I thought by going through with this marriage, that would happen.

Having never really proposed to me, my boyfriend and I went looking for wedding rings. He didn't have a job since returning from the states, so I had to purchase our rings. And again y'all, this was something that totally went against what I had in mind. All the movies I'd seen showed the man buying the ring, getting down on one knee in the middle of dreamy scenery, and popping the "would you marry me?" question. Nah, none of that happened in my reality.

No one from my family knew I was even getting married. Why? Because my mom decided to cut communication with me because I told her I was pregnant. My father was nowhere in the picture so he never knew the type of man that would take his daughter's hand in marriage. I didn't have any girlfriends to relish in the moments of picking out a dress or preparing a tasting party for the wedding cake. None of that. Just me, him, and our unborn baby in the Post Exchange (PX, military store) picking out wedding rings.

I was nine months pregnant when we exchange vows. I had never attended a wedding nor did I know what to do. Neither one of us had prepared our vows. I had on a borrowed dress from one of the ladies at the church. After what seemed like an eternity, we were married.

We both started attending the church we were married in. This was also the same church I first attended in the white dress. I had since surrendered my life to Christ, thanks to the help and prayers of my then good friend, John. My new husband attended because he knew that's what I wanted and he got tired of hearing me nag him about it. A little over two weeks after getting married, I gave birth to our beautiful daughter, Kimarra.

The whole ordeal played out so fast. I went into the hospital thinking I was going to push her from my body. After being in labor for twenty-four hours, the doctors had to make a last minute decision to do an emergency C-section due to my daughter's condition.

When I woke up from surgery, my baby lied next to me sound asleep in her little bed. My face washed with hot with tears as I watched that little person sleeping. She was mine. She was my daughter. I was her mother. God had entrusted this broken vessel to raise and nurture another life. I vowed to do my best.

13

And So, It Begins

"Dear brothers and sisters, when troubles of any kind
come your way, consider it an opportunity for great joy."
– James 1:2, New Living Translation

Many times, we are oblivious to the tests before us. We go along our way or make that decision not knowing the potential bite that awaits. That's what happened with the Samaritan woman. Only her test turned out to be of utter importance, hence here we are two thousand years later still talking about her life. It turned out that the validity of her life would be tested and put on display for her to see.

The love I had for my daughter grew exponentially. I didn't realize this love resonated so deep within me. Every time I looked at her beautiful face, I remembered back when I sat in my dogwood tree and vowed to never treat my "future" children anything like I had been treated. Even though I despised kids, I still made myself a promise that should I ever have any, they would know what it meant to have a great, loved, and well nurtured life,

#coffeemoments
As long as the roots of my past still rested in the grounds of my heart, I would only be making vain attempts at getting life right and eventually, spread those roots right into the delicate parts of her life.

It took time for me to get used to someone else depending on me. I wanted so desperately to ensure that my baby saw the best of me. I wanted to give her the best. And as much as I wanted to and even attempted to, what I didn't realize was.

I attempted to make the old apartment as cozy as possible. Since I wasn't that high in rank, I didn't have enough money to purchase good furniture. But I had amazing people in my unit. My squad leader gave me her entire living room set since she purchased a new one. A co-worker bought a crib set for the little one. And several other people pitched in to purchase other necessities for my apartment. My First Sergeant bought so many baby supplies that lasted until my baby turned six months! Yes, I was truly loved by my unit. As much as I felt the love from my unit, I couldn't exactly say the same thing about my marriage.

Our marriage was still fresh in the honeymoon stage, but it was already hanging on by threads. We kept at each other's throats. Frustrations grew because my husband had yet to find a job since returning from the states.

One day, after coming in from physical training (PT), I had had it. As I went into our room, there he laid in bed watching television, with the baby laying in her car seat carrier at the foot of the bed. I was done, y'all.

I asked was he going to lay around, smoke, and watch tv all day instead of looking for a job. He spat some curse words out, but the one curse word that came out of his mouth got an instant reaction. He called me out of my name.

Now, I don't know about you, but I'm not one of those women who likes being called out of her name. I'm not going to walk around and just let anyone call me anything. I had grown out of that. Before I knew it, I had slapped him hard across the face and told him he better not ever call me out of my name again. He jumped up and grabbed me by my PT jacket and slammed me up next to the bedroom window. He growled that he would throw my (several expletives) out of the window.

We lived on the second floor, a very tall, long distance second floor I might add. Very calmly, I said if he did he better make sure I died because if I lived, I was going to gut him like a fish. From seeing my mom's experience with men beating on her, I made a vow that I'd kill a man before he had the opportunity to do that to me.

Yes, he was the father of my child, but I couldn't live with myself knowing that I allowed a man to put his hands on me. I may have been a push over, but only to a certain point. I had a temper that went underestimated because of my timid side. Years of deep-seated rage rested inside me and it was starting to bubble to the surface.

He put me down and went on ranting and raving through the apartment. I didn't want to get into trouble being that I was the servicemember and my husband was the civilian. So, I grabbed my baby's car seat and headed out of the apartment. She screamed through the entire ordeal. Even with her being so little, my intentions were to never expose her to that level of violence, ever.

My supervisor got involved and asked what I wanted to do. The regulations stated that I would have to leave the premises because I was the servicemember. Over my dead body. I wasn't going anywhere without my child. To this day, I don't know how I was able to stay, but I did. He ended up staying at one of his friend's houses for a little while.

Even though we had threatened each other's lives, the little time he was away, my heart ached. That picture of a perfect family was at the forefront of my mind. No matter what I did to make life what I envisioned, the pieces would always remain scattered until I owned my truth.

#coffeemoments
What I didn't know at the time, was how my dysfunction and brokenness had attracted an equally dysfunctional and broken person.

As if that red flag wasn't enough to grab my attention, the next time around included an obvious exit sign. That sign came when I tried receiving military pay entitlements for being married and having dependents. I found out that my marriage certificate was no good because the pastor who married us wasn't authorized to do so in Europe. We planned to go to the local courthouse and legitimize the marriage (Justice of the Peace). So, in other words, technically our marriage never existed and we were co-habiting (shacking up) for some time.

The day we showed up to the courthouse, we both were angry at each other. We had on our work uniforms and sat on opposite ends of the very large, decorative room. Where high spirits and love should have been in the air, instead vibes of aggravation and frustration set in. The judicial officer walked through the doors with a jolly smile on his face. The smile quickly disappeared when he felt the vibes in the room and saw the looks on our faces. He hesitantly greeted us and gave instructions on how things were to go. I stood with my arms crossed, rolling my eyes. *"Why am I going through with this?"* was all that kept going through my mind. After an awkward silence, the judicial officer asked if we were sure we wanted to go through with this. Yes, really, he did. I know we looked a hot mess standing in front of that man. I said, "Sir, can we just get this over with so I can go back to work?" We half-heartedly exchanged vows and put the rings back on our fingers. We sat down and signed some papers then it was over and done. He went his way and I went mine.

My frustrations grew because while I tried to make myself better for my new family, my husband was still stuck in the single life mentality. He had finally gotten a job but took it for granted. He stayed out late and hung around the wrong crowd.

We continued going to church together, but had since started attending a new church. We left the previous church due to a bitter church split. That happened while I was out on maternity leave. I had never experienced a church split before, so with most of the members gone, we left too and hopped around different churches. Being that I was still stationed in Germany, finding the right church was very limited. But we eventually found one. I thought that by us attending church, that would straighten out the kinks in our marriage. What I didn't know was that it took a whole lot more than checking off the block of going to church to make a marriage work.

September 11, 2001 came like a bad nightmare. I was in the middle of completing a pile of inprocessing packets for incoming soldiers. Tired was an understatement. I was ready to go home and see my baby girl. Suddenly, a loud voice came over the intercom in the entire building stating that the facility had been placed on "threatcon Delta." That meant there was imminent danger for United States citizens and military personnel.

At first, I'm not going to lie, I was a bit irritated. Again, I had had a long day and was ready to make this hour long trip home to my baby girl. But when as I walked up to the lobby and looked at what was on the screen, fear overtook any ounce of anger I had.

Everyone seemed to be frozen in time. We stood silent as we watched the second plane crash into the World Trade Center. It looked like a scene from a very good action movie. Bodies were captured on camera as they fell from high levels of the towers. I sunk down in a chair and covered my face. I never anticipated something like this ever happening while I was in the military. Okay, in my very, very naïve train of thought, I figured it was safe to join the Army. Desert Storm was over and there had been peace and silence in the years that followed. Only, the truth was, silence never was. Plots and plans were brewing the entire time. And the product of those plots and plans carried out for the entire world to see. The United States had just been ambushed by terrorists. We were under attack.

The next year of my life was a whirlwind of training and preparation. Safe no longer existed in military. We all had become targets of one of the world's largest terrorist groups and now we were preparing to fight back.

I barely had the chance to see my daughter. Between long hours at work, sometimes being locked down, and long hours pulling gate guard, I knew I was missing out on a lot with her. The childcare development centers or CDC, carried a lot of responsibility of raising and rearing my daughter. The frustrations in my marriage only built up higher and higher. Since my schedule for gate guard required I work four days and nights straight, we ended up having Fridays off. By the time I got home, I was exhausted and didn't want to be bothered, didn't want to cook, didn't want to hang out with my husband. Having to be in one high stressful environment only to come home to another one, was not what was up. So, I slowly turned back to drinking and eventually going out again.

My girls and I hit the club frequently. We partied like rock stars, bringing the sun up. They were my club partners but also my shoulders to cry on and ears to vent to. They knew the blows my marriage was taking, but through it all they never once criticized me for choosing to stay with him (if you're reading this ladies, just know y'all are my sisters for life).

February 2003, my unit received word that we were deploying that next month to Iraq. We had been called in on an alert; it was two o'clock in the morning when we were told the news. All color drained from my face. It was one thing to have to pull long hours of gate guard and prepare. It was a whole other playing field to hear that we were actually going to a foreign and very dangerous country. All kinds of thoughts crossed my mind. The first ones being, what about my baby? And what in the world would finance soldiers do? We were paper pushers who were good with numbers and money!

Another whirlwind blew right threw my life and before I knew it, we were leaving. Y'all, leaving family was one thing, but not knowing if I was going to return created a different narrative altogether. I cried until I had no more tears left. I felt like my heart was being ripped from my chest leaving my daughter. She was barely two years old. We had just pulled up in front of my unit in the wee hours of the morning. My husband fought back tears as he unpacked all my gear from the trunk.

The flight across continents was long and painstakingly uncomfortable. Thank goodness, we had the opportunity to fly on a commercial flight. The civilians on board showered us with their gratitude for us fighting for their freedom and safety. For a split second, I felt like we were in the middle of a war movie scene. I was brought back to reality when I heard the voice of one of the flight attendants across the speaker. Through soft sobs, she thanked us all for our service and said how brave we were for what we signed up to do. She then said, "And we'll be right here waiting for you after you've served overseas for two years." She said it with sincerity as she smiled through tears. I'm sure she only thought she was making us feel better. But all we could hear was "two years." In instant confusion and the panicked looks on our faces, the flight attendant asked if she had said something wrong. We said yes indeed she did, we were not staying in Iraq for two years, unless we missed a huge memo! Our commander corrected the attendant and said we'd only be there for nine months. With relieved laughter, we all sighed and laughed. She profusely apologized for scaring us. Yes ma'am, as if we weren't scared enough already.

We touched down in Kuwait late that night. I couldn't believe the freezing temperatures as we headed over to a huge briefing tent we called the "circus" tent because of its size. After receiving briefings from the officials, they also warned us of the different signals of attack. Truthfully, I glazed through half of the briefing. All I could think of was eating and going to sleep.

Our temporary living quarters for the first few nights was another large circus tent. I guess Kuwait wanted to give us a welcome we'd never forget by blowing in a monster sand storm that night. A few minutes before the storm ensued, my whole unit laid in our cots (if you're not familiar with what that is, refer to the television show, M.A.S.H.), with flashlights pinging off the roof of the tent. The winds were violently shaking everything around us. My homegirls were next to me looking up at the rooftop as well. After one of us voiced our concern about the stakes being deep enough into the ground to secure the tent, the wind proved to us those stakes were no match for its force.

The tent was completely yanked up on one side, revealing what looked like a massive cloud, only that cloud was slicing sand. Besides wet dirt that used to cut my knees back home (yes, I was a little mud guppy), I had never felt sand cut like that before.

Our supervisors yelled for us to cover our faces. We covered with face masks, bandanas, t-shirts, and pretty much anything we could find. The storm moved in, blocking out any ounce of light. We worked in pitch black darkness, trying to regain control of the tent. After what seemed like forever, we were finally able to stabilize the tent again. When we got light, we weren't prepared for what we saw. Everyone looked like we played in nothing but flour. Our belongings looked like they hadn't been dusted in years. Sand piles were everywhere. Welcome to the middle east.

Over the course of nine months of being away from my family, I changed. From the traumatic kidnapping of Private First Class (PFC) Jessica Lynch to me witnessing from the rooftop of my building, the fire fight between the United States military and Sadaam Hussein's sons, my life changed forever. The environment I temporarily lived in brought out a dark side of me I didn't know existed. Having seen and smelled the stench of burning flesh and just being around death and negativity, transformed me. When I returned, I most definitely wasn't the same timid, bend over backwards Lucrecia as before.

The club and alcohol became my new best friends. All my stress, worries, doubts, disappeared when I hit the dance floor. I absolutely craved and loved the attention I got from men when I wore revealing outfits or cat suits. Thanks to being deployed for such a long time with sucky food, I was able to create the body I wanted. And you better believe I showed it off every chance I got. When my girlfriends and I stepped into the club, from the bar to the floor I went. I danced to get attention. My moves were very provocative because I knew I could have any man I wanted, so I thought. At the end of every venture, I hated to return home to the wreck

I called my marriage. My husband also developed a habit of going out a lot. We both figured the best way to get through the night with each other was to club up as much of the night as possible. One of our family friends watched our daughter since she had a little one herself.

One morning as I was nursing hangover, my husband and I had gotten into a horrible argument. He returned home smelling like pounds of weed. My friend had not long ago dropped our daughter off and she was sound asleep in her room. As much as I tried keeping the argument down, it didn't work.

We were neck deep in the argument. "Well how bout we just get a divorce then?" my husband said as he stood and waited for my usual response of crying and begging him not to leave. But my reply shocked him. "Let's go then! I was supposed to have divorced you a long time ago anyway!" I shot back. He didn't see that one coming. A look of confusion crossed his face. Who was this woman standing in front of him? Why, all of a sudden, had I decided to become confident? Why? Because I was different.

My marriage was on fire (and not in a good way). The fire was burning everything in sight. We couldn't communicate without flaming. We couldn't be in the same room with each other for more than five minutes without flaming. We wore our petty hats day and night, trying to one up the next person or make the other person feel so bad and low. We tore at the chords of our marriage so much that all was left was tattered pieces.

And while we tried to stick it out even through the brokenness and dysfunction, we didn't realize our daughter suffered just as much. She had gotten used to us arguing. So much so, that as she got older and realized we were arguing, she excused herself into her room where she became accustomed to staying.

Sisters, here's the sad truth. When we go through issues with our significant other and there's children involved, if we're not careful we can completely neglect them.

#coffeemoments
We push our children off to the side so we can continue with our selfish, vindictive agendas.

Being at work relieved me. It was my stress-free place, a place where I laughed and enjoyed being around other people. We were a tight-knit crew who truly had each other's backs.

I grew especially close to one of my co-workers. Every day was a clowning session in the office, whether it was us clowning each other or the customers who came in. We ate lunch together almost daily. He listened to me as I vented about my husband. He listened to me gripe about going home and how the only reason I was going home was because of my daughter. He gave me his ear to blast out and shoulder to cry on. He became my comfortable, safe place.

NOTE There should NEVER be a time when we (married ladies) become okay or comfortable with talking to another man (who isn't our husband), married or single, about our marital problems!

At first, I was oblivious to what was developing. All I knew was that I enjoyed talking to someone who understood me. I enjoyed his company and how he made me feel so good, pretty, and like a woman. Over time, we grew closer, sharing deeper, more intimate thoughts and dreams with each other. My co-workers had a hint of what was developing but chose not to say anything to us about it.

I started making excuses to my husband just so I could stay at work late. When we left, he'd call me just to make sure I got home safe. My heart started fluttering in a way I had never experience before in adulthood. I became smitten by him. We started connecting emotionally.

One blistering cold day, I decided to linger a little longer in the office. All my work had been completed but I just wanted to stay and chill with my co-worker. He finished his work and came inside the main office where I was. We laughed and talked about everything. Neither of us realized how late it had gotten so we decided to end the conversation. Light snow had started to fall and a weather update came across the radio about "black ice." I didn't know the first thing about ice or snow since I was from Florida. My first time ever seeing snow was when I arrived in Germany. I was like a little kid sitting on Santa's lap. I stuck my tongue out, ran around, made snow angels, everything I could think of just to relish in the snow. But over time, I learned how much of a nuisance snow could be.

Beautiful but sometimes a pain.

By the time the weather report ended, my co-worker and I had moved closer to each other. He grabbed my hand and began expressing to me some of the fantasies he had in his mind of the two of us. He invited me to his house since he lived only a few minutes away. Everything in me burned to go. Without warning, he grabbed me in his arms and hugged me tightly. He was very tall so he knelt and whispered in my ear to come back to his place. I fought hard with everything in me to tell him no because my body was screaming yes. Emotionally, he had me. He had touched me in areas that had never been touched before. I was willing to let go of my marriage to be with him. I yearned to be stimulated daily with his presence. But I couldn't, for the sake of my daughter, I couldn't.

I backed away from him and said I had to go before I gave in. He smiled and let me know his door was always open. Without looking back at him, I hopped in my Grand Jeep Cherokee and hurried out of the parking lot. I blasted my girl crush, Mary J. Blige's "Without You." Sisters, if you didn't know already, when you're in a bad emotional mindset, the last thing to do is blast music that will pacify your mood. Only makes things worse!

As I was driving down the autobahn or highway, I was howling Mary's words when I felt my steering wheel give slightly. I didn't pay much attention to it until the next few seconds, my wheels gave again. This time I couldn't control my steering wheel. Going about eighty miles per hour, I swerved across the busy highway. I desperately tried to regain control of my truck but I had no idea how to fight the black ice. The left front side of my truck slammed into the guard rail which caused my truck to ricochet. From the hard impact, the back of my truck slammed into the same guard rail and I spun out of control across the autobahn. Panicking and screaming, I mashed the brakes as hard as I could. I even pulled up the emergency brake but nothing stopped the truck from barreling into oncoming traffic across the median. Helpless, I watched as my truck sped recklessly across the frozen, grassy median.

Suddenly, I felt a hard jolt as if something in front of my truck stopped it. My head hit the steering wheel as the back of my truck lifted and slammed hard back to the ground. Silence and smoke. I raised my throbbing head from the steering wheel and looked around. Traffic continued flowing down the highway. Not one other car was hit or effected by my out of control vehicle. How did I not hit another vehicle and another vehicle not crash into me? But God...

Screaming, I grabbed my cell phone. I wish I could tell you the first person I called was my husband, but it wasn't. It was the guy. I screamed in the phone what happened and I heard the panic in his voice as he said he would be right there. After I got off the phone with him, I got out of the truck to look at the damage.

Deep, dark skid marks trailed from the highway through the frozen grass. I was only a few feet from the other side of the highway towards oncoming traffic. I looked at the speeding vehicles and noticed another one of my friends from work fly by. I could see his head look back and his brake lights came on. I could tell he was going to find a way to turn around and come see about me. Still clutching my phone, I called my husband and told him what happened. He asked if I was okay and he didn't know if he'd be able to get out of work but would try. A few minutes later, the Polizei (German Police Officers) came to the scene. They checked everything out and were very surprised to see my accident only involved one vehicle. My friend had made his way back to the scene as well. He jumped out to see if I was okay. Not far behind him was my pursuer. Trying hard to keep feelings under wraps, he rubbed my shoulder and comforted me. I opted to not go to the hospital because I didn't feel like spending the whole night there. friend said he would take me home since he had to go to the commissary back in town.

My accident was long behind me, but my relationship with my co-worker continued. You would've thought that the accident would've shaken me to my senses, but it didn't. In my mind, he was everything. My emotions warped my perspective. What I saw on the other side seemed way greener than where I currently was. I wanted what was on the other side. I no longer wanted to play around in secret. I was ready to be free and happy.

14

A Broken Mess

"He found me in my mess, that's where He found me."
– Uncle Reece

When Jesus told the woman to go and get her husband, I wonder what her physical response was. I mean, she knew the truth but this "man" didn't or so she presumed. When she responded with "I don't have a husband," that was the turning point to her entire life. What the woman didn't realize was Jesus knew all along the history of her past. He knew she was a broken mess. And He knew He would use that mess and turn it into her ministry. The lives of the very people who shunned and outcasted her, depended on the transformation of her encounter with Jesus and the transformation of her mess.

My time in the military had come to an end. I had been in Germany for almost eight years. I had my times of traveling to amazing countries, such as Denmark, France (twice), and my absolute favorite Italy. I was so blessed to have had the opportunity to travel to places for so cheap and live out my childhood dreams. I made some of the most amazing friends. But as much as I loved Europe, I was done and ready to touch U.S. soil again, for good. Traveling back and forth from Europe to the United States was fun but I was ready to live somewhere in the states.

#coffeemoments
Secrets have a way of seeping out. When we think we have them well concealed, they tend to find a way out and tell all our business.

The packing process was stressful enough, but we also carried and packed up the broken pieces of our marriage and traveled with it across the Atlantic Ocean. Though I was so ready to divorce my husband, I still carried the thoughts of my mom's broken life and how much I did not want to be her. I also carried the secret of my affair across continents. Ladies, let me highlight something quickly. How do I know? Because that's exactly what happened to me.

Since we had never celebrated our honeymoon, we decided to take a trip to Jamaica for seven days. We left Kimarra in New York with her grandmother and flew out from there down to Jamaica. I was hoping that by being out of the country would help us to get along at least a little bit. It didn't. Jamaica was gorgeous and exotic, but we could barely enjoy ourselves for arguing almost the entire time. I so wished that trip could have been different, but I was ready to go back to the states. I no longer wanted to explore anything for one more day, although because I'm a foodie, I truly wish I could've brought some ox tails, lima beans, and rice back.

After packing up from my husband's mother's house, we made our way to the airport for another flight to Texas. We touched down at the San Antonio International airport in June 2006. I was used to the heat in my home state of Florida. I had experienced hell-fire heat in Iraq. Surprisingly, the heat I felt in Texas was equally hot. But the city was beautiful. I instantly fell in love with San Antonio. I know you're probably wondering how we ended up in Texas to begin with, being that neither of us are from there. Well, I felt we were spiritually lead. It sounds a bit contradictory to say we were spiritually lead when our lives had been ransacked by mess. But God has His ways and they always come through.

On the outside looking in at our family, things looked great. We seemed like the ideal family living in the ideal neighborhood. I worked at a very large banking corporation and my husband had a good paying job as well. Oh, how deceiving smokescreens are! They give the illusion of one thing when it's something completely different brewing. We fought constantly. Our daughter got caught in the middle of several of our blowouts.

Because I felt that some of our blowouts were due to my emotional relationship to the guy in Germany, I made the decision to cut things off with him. It was painful because at this point, he had professed his love for me. I felt like me cutting him off had ripped his heart out of his chest, jabbed it a few times, then handed it back to him. But the truth was, he couldn't be mine and I couldn't be his. After ending the relationship, I started back going to church.

I went through the motions of surrendering parts of my life back to God but I didn't surrender my whole life. I preserved a part of me for the "just in case" moments. Y'all get what I'm saying, I'm sure. In addition to rekindling my relationship with God, I decided to try and make things work again within my marriage. And of course, when it rains it pours.

Not long after I rededicated myself back to God, my husband was fired from his job. With him being home all the time and me working at a very stressful job placed unnecessary weight on my shoulders. He had a lot of time on his hands which lead to deep secrets making their entrance into our lives. Our marriage was in more trouble. Quite honestly, I don't see how it ever continued for as long as it did.

Then we plummeted into debt. We both maxed out credit cards, overdrew our bank accounts by hundreds trying to rob Pete to pay Paul. The stress started reflecting in my performance at my job. My manager rode my tail every chance she got.

I was over it all. Tired of fighting for my marriage and getting nowhere. Tired of working for a job that caused me to break out in hives and develop a nervous twitch. Tired of swimming in debt. Tired of living an unfulfilled, empty life. My mom had shut me out her life again. At that point, I had gotten used to it; it didn't make me feel any better though. I was just tired.

Wednesday after Wednesday and Sunday after Sunday, we attended church. I was desperately hopeful that at one of those church services, I would hear a good word from God, that right now word. One Wednesday night in particular, I did not want to go to bible study. I was still in my "I'm over it" mindset. But we went anyway. My church had started a new thing called small groups, so when we got there everyone was already divided up into groups. I barely knew anyone in that church, I guess thanks to my antisocialism.

The usher greeted us and guided us over to a group at the far side of the church. My mind was everywhere but on the topic of discussion. Open discussions started and I sat quietly as everyone else engaged in conversation. Then one young lady raised her hand. She had to be no older than eighteen years old. I'll never forget her inquiry.

She asked how could she maintain her Christianity when she attended college. She had just graduated high school and wanted to try to stay as closely as possible to her spiritual foundation. But she was a bit concerned because of what she heard about college. The answers I heard were so far over my head. And if they were over mine, then I knew for sure they were over that young lady's head. One lady almost sounded as if she were rebuking the girl for even asking the question.

I had since come out of my conscious coma and was now fully attentive to this conversation. I suddenly felt a heat sensation come over me, starting in my belly. I raised my hand and stood up. Y'all, this was so not me! I would never do that. Now, I know it was the Holy Spirit guiding me, but then I just thought I had temporarily lost my mind.

I answered the girl with what was placed in my heart to say. I told her of my experience in the military and how though it wasn't college, several of us were her age. I told her the importance of being honest with God on her journey and how when she reached those weak moments, to reach out to someone back here, and to pray. I said other things that I can't recall right now, but I was floored as I listened to myself. I could barely take my own advice. Where did this advice come from and how did I ever

#coffeemoments
Now I know, the advice came directly from the Holy Spirit and I wasn't qualified, but at that moment God

feel qualified enough to give it to that young lady? Even with me having the Holy Spirit, I still felt disqualified to help anyone because of my own battles with sin. The young lady responded with a smile of gratitude and thanked me for my honesty. She looked a lot more calm and relaxed than she did when she was being excommunicated by the other ladies.

Later that night, as I stood in the shower letting the water glaze over my tired body, I felt a rush of heat. I thought it was the water so I adjusted the knobs. The heat remained and deep within me, I heard a faint whisper. It was the Holy Spirit. The voice was faint but very clear. "You need to go back into the military."

Y'all, I jumped out of that shower so quick! I almost broke my ankle trying to clear the tub as I grabbed hold of my towel. My husband was sitting on the bed watching sports. He glanced over at me then did a double take because of the bewildered look I had on my face. I told him what I had heard in the shower and he objected. He felt that it should be him to go back in. I told him I knew what I had heard and that I wasn't crazy. Besides, I had already been pondering the thoughts of going back into the Army. I felt unfulfilled, like I left some goals unmet. I knew in my heart of hearts that I heard God correctly. I had some work to do, namely, to lose the weight.

Since I was no longer confined to the strict regulations of the military concerning weight, I gave myself some wiggle room and welcomed some "love" (that's what I like to call fat). I met with a recruiter who said I had a good chance of reenlisting since I hadn't been out that long. Literally, it was like I was on a super long vacation from the Army. I was out for only a year and three months before I reenlisted.

I worked hard to drop those extra pounds I packed on. Working out two to three times a day and eating low carb crash diets pushed me to my goal. Upon reenlisting, I was awarded a very generous bonus, one I had no idea I was entitled to.

This time around felt different. The first time I enlisted into the Army, I was a scared, naïve seventeen-year-old kid. Now here I was, a full-grown woman with responsibilities. My options were very skimpy, one including a tour in Korea. I told the recruiter I would most certainly pass on that one since I spent almost eight years in Europe. My only other stateside option was Fort Campbell, Kentucky. My heart skipped some beats. Not because I was happy and excited, but because I had heard horror stories about that place. They were hard core. But I chose it. One chapter closed another one about to open.

The saying "it's a small world" is so true, especially in the military. When, at first, I felt like a complete stranger, that changed quickly when I arrived at my unit. I saw many familiar faces from my old unit in Germany. Seeing them eased my anxiety. Apparently, they had word of my arrival because when I walked through the doors of the office, my new squad leader approached me. He said he had already been briefed on my expertise in finance and was glad to have me be a part of his team. I mentioned earlier that I really loved my job as a financial analyst. Well, thankfully I got to keep that same job and rank when I reenlisted. To say that I loved my job was an understatement. I lived, breathed, and ate finance. I was awful at math, but for some reason, when it came to military pay, I got it. My favorite part about my job was hunting down debts and scoping out the people who were receiving entitlements they weren't entitled to. You could say I was like an investigator. So, to hear how my professional reputation proceeded me, made me very proud.

I was immediately put to work. The love for my job was instantly rekindled. It wasn't long before I was placed second in charge in the office. Things at work seemed to flow well. At home, was a different story. We lived on post and our apartment was very small and ridiculously old. It was tested monthly for asbestos and lead (like, really, and they had us living there?) It was difficult to make that place cozy but I did the best I could. My daughter had been transferred to another school at the beginning of the school year so she started 1st grade on post. My husband got a job working on post as well.

> #coffeemoments
> No matter how hard we try ladies, as long as we keep ourselves bound down by the lies and smokescreens, we will never be free.

Unfortunately, we carried the weight and strain of our marriage to Fort Campbell. All that external stuff, you know, the fun, laughter, trips, money, etc., all are just good props to reality. And that reality will travel wherever you and I go until we decide to deal with it.

We played the roles so well, y'all. We had people fooled into thinking we were so crazily in love with each other. We even had the audacity to talk about other couples and how their marriages were failing. All the while, ours sat on a brewing volcano. I've noticed through my life how easy it is to point the finger at someone else's flaw but fail to realize there are four other fingers pointing back at me.

People noticed how late I stayed at work or the gym. At first, they chalked it up to me just being a dedicated soldier and health buff. Which I was. But one morning, the truth of my reality tumbled out.

I drove up to my place of duty that morning, and just sat in my car. My eyes were swollen from heavy crying and my throat was extremely sore from yelling. I had just left a very bad argument at my apartment. My husband and I nearly threw blows at each other before I took off. It was during PT (physical training) and it was mandatory to show up, unless we had an authorized excuse. I say authorized because some people really tried to pull fast ones just to get out of working out.

I sat in my car until I saw my detachment sergeant come out of the building. He always was the last one to come out of our office. I had grown very fond of him, we all did. He was like our dad. This hefty, burly Caucasian with a Minnesota accent that came out from time to time, he was one of the coolest humans I had ever met. He cursed us out when we did wrong, but felt so bad about it, spent the rest of the day explaining why he had to do it.

When he saw me coming, he stopped in his tracks. He asked what was wrong and I explained through sobs. He wanted to ensure that I hadn't been hit, I reassured him that I hadn't been hit or I'd be speaking to him from behind bars. He told me to go inside his office and just cool off and that I didn't have to come back out for PT. I felt so relieved because I didn't feel like facing the eyeballs or answering questions. When PT was over, I left. Before I got to my car, my detachment sergeant stopped me and gave me some sound advice. He said that some things are worth it and others aren't and that I needed to be able to decipher the two. If only I had taken him at his advice then.

15

The Set Up

"And we know that God causes everything to work together for the good of those who love God and are called according to His purpose for them." ---Romans 8:28, New Living Translation

The woman had no idea at all that meeting Jesus at the well was all a set up. She didn't know that her life would be the catalyst to a generational transformation. She didn't know that over 2,000 years later, her life would still be talked about and would greatly impact lives today. The woman at the well may have counted herself out of anything worthy, but God counted her as qualified and worthy. She was His masterpiece and He would use every part of her life for His good use.

I was preparing for my next deployment or "rendezvous with destiny" as deployments were known at Ft. Campbell. Deployments really didn't come as a surprise since this installation was known for frequent deployments. The season of life I was in wasn't the best and separation from my husband would prove damaging.

My unit left January 2009. The nation had since learned in November of the previous year that it would welcome a very different president, Barak Obama. When the news hit my ears that he won the election, my heart fluttered. Never did I think the United States of America would see its first African American President. I couldn't imagine the major impact this moment had on the older African American generation. To witness something like this was incredible.

We touched down in Iraq again at night. Hungry was an understatement.

We were *"hangry."* We were briefed on all protocols in the dangerous country. A lot had changed since the last time I'd been there, but the danger remained the same. The war-torn country had been built up and better established from the six years I first entered the country.

After the briefings, we were released to the dining facility (DFAC). I was not expecting that amazing aroma floating from the doors as we neared the facility. Those cooks were doing the most (in a good way) and truly blessing my nose.

As we entered, the facility was beautiful and there were flat-screened televisions all around. Every channel was on CNN. And on that channel, was the inauguration ceremony for Barak Obama. Motionless, many of us stood still and watched in awe.

I get it, we were soldiers and were trained to withhold emotion. But seeing this went deeper for me. Someone who looked like me, my family, my generation, stood on the podium swearing to uphold all that was required as the President of the United States. Tears silently rolled down my cheeks as I watched. Floods of pride overcame my body as I had never felt prouder to serve my country.

With the President's last words, the dining facility erupted into cheering and clapping. Our 44th President of the United States had officially taken office. I thought that set things into motion for this to be the beginning of a good rest of the deployment for us. Wrong.

One of the unfortunate downfalls about leadership is that sometimes everyone thinks they're a leader. Communication was screwed up. Leaders did what they wanted without considering the consequences. Morale was very low. I looked forward to going to my little cozy room every night just to get away from it all.

Our living quarters weren't blown out buildings, debris, or riddled with animal carcasses. Instead, we had decent looking trailers. Since the area had been developed over the course of time, we were able to purchase items for our rooms and decorate.

I became very good friends with one of my co-workers a few months before we deployed. Her and I were assigned as roommates for the duration of the deployment. Both of us were girly, loved smelling good, and were pretty good hustlers. So, we hustled for a lot of our furniture and amenities. Every time we had room inspections, our leadership always wondered how we got the things we had. We had the gift of the hustle.

Something else my "sister friend" and I had in common was that we both loved looking good. Yes, even in the dessert we were going to keep ourselves looking right. Being deployed in the middle east was no excuse for uncombed hair, dingy uniforms, and just a sloppy look. And our efforts got us a lot of attention, not that we were looking for it. Being away from home for long periods of time did something to the eye. What may have not been so attractive back home, suddenly looked like a McDonald's #2 in the dessert.

There were only a handful of African American women in my detachment, so we stuck together. We became very well-known at our camp amongst the foreign workers and other military personnel. I'm not going to lie, the attention pumped me up a bit. It had been a very long time that I actually felt like I still "had it." So, when I started noticing guys noticing me, I entertained it. The mentality I had in my younger years came back. Only this time, it was sprinkled with some experience. I knew how to handle guys to my advantage.

A little disclaimer: Here's the nasty and ugly truth about deployments, some people are influenced to commit acts they probably wouldn't normally commit back home. The availability and opportunity to do so is high. And infidelity was an opportunity and it came knocking at my door. And I answered.

I was caught at a weak moment. No excuse at all, this is just the truth. I left home with my marriage literally hanging on by a thread. I told my husband we were pretty much done when I got back because I was just tired. Tired of digging the trenches deeper and deeper around the same mountain. Tired of wearing him out and him wearing me out.

#coffeemoments
It's truly amazing how deception disguises itself into making us believe it's really on our side.

I had once again, fallen into the trap of getting too comfortable with sharing my marital issues with another guy. And not just any guy, but one who was packaged just right. Ladies, please heed this warning. *Satan is not and will not send anyone or anything your way he knows will not entice you. He will always package that gift up to look, feel, smell, sound, and taste exactly how you dreamed. He'll even go as far as to making that thing or person almost seem right.* Discernment and a solid relationship with God and self are vital. I allowed my flesh to entertain and get the best of me and committed the sin of adultery. Aside from the horrible line I crossed with the physical part of the affair, I had a very bad feeling that something was going to happen, that this one was going to haunt me.

It was towards the end of the deployment and it was time to gear up to face reality again. Because being deployed wasn't it, reality I mean. Yeah, we were faced with real danger and the constant threat of death, but for some, being deployed was a getaway/vacation from real life. So, it was time to put our reality hats on again. I was eager to see my nine-year-old daughter. My heart ached every time a new picture was sent to me and I saw her emotionless face. Her eyes looked so empty. And for a whole year, I felt helpless to fill that void. No matter how many stuffed animals I sent or letters I wrote, it was nothing in comparison to my actual presence.

We got back to the states January 2010. From the moment my dusty boot hit the ground, my life shifted, again. That bad feeling I had just before I left Iraq, greeted me with open arms. Things went from bad to worse in a split second. While my unit reintegrated back into normal society, I was scheduling appointments with a divorce lawyer. I believe my husband and I were toxic to each other. The longer we stayed together, the more we poisoned each other and inadvertently poisoned our daughter.

That season of my life was unbearable. I had to pretend and fake the funk each and every day. Putting on that uniform posed as a big mask for what was going on behind closed doors. I had hit a three-foot-thick brick wall, but no one ever knew. Because I knew how to act well. My persona or alter ago name was "Boss Lady." My soldiers gave me that name because of my ability to handle things and get the job done. They used to say, "SGT Ruffin, we're going to start calling you 'Boss Lady' because of the way you handle your business." And while that alter ego was perfected in the professional world, my personal world was crumbling fast.

Remnants of the affair carried over from the middle east to the states and all hell broke loose in my life. I lost friends, respect, dignity in myself and my character was badly tarnished. I went into a huge depression. To this day, I still can't even tell you how I was able to maintain myself at work. My life was hell. I fought every night with demons tormenting my mind. Sleep became a wish more than a reality. And to top things off, my husband had been served his divorce papers and he was not happy at all. I had also found out that he was doing his own dirt on the side while I was gone, but that didn't stop him from making this divorce as difficult as he possibly could.

I could take the heat he tossed my way until he threatened to take my daughter from me. The mama bear had been pushed against the wall. Over my dead body. He had listened to his homeboys and was ready to dispute the divorce. I was ready too. Because of my job in the military, I knew exactly how these situations worked. My job was my classroom and I learned all there was to know about military personnel and divorces.

It had been three months since being back home and I lived in the guest room of the home my husband and I bought together before I deployed. That was the first time I had ever lived in that home besides the two weeks I returned mid-deployment for R & R. The decision to purchase a new home together haunted me all the way up until a few months ago (literally).

Before I deployed, I realized we had outgrown the apartment we lived in on post since my youngest sister decided to come live with us and our dog, a German Rottweiler, had grown very big. And since his breed was considered vicious, many homeowners refused to allow us to rent from them. I can't lie and say I was all in about the decision to purchase a home because I wasn't. Our marriage was in no shape prepared for something like buying a house together.

Reluctantly, I went through with it. I had to go through my supervisor to have some documents signed to approve the financial part of the home. He hesitated and went back and forth about signing the documents because he knew the nature of my marriage. I remember him asking me several times if I was sure about doing this and that I could always wait until I returned to decide if we still wanted to go through with purchasing the house. In other words, my supervisor was trying to get me to smell the coffee and wake up. He was trying to prevent me from going into something that could potentially bite my backside hard in the long run. But I thought about the dog and the comfort of my daughter and sister while I was gone. And again, I went on through with the decision.

Boy, boy, boy hindsight 20/20 truly is a beast when you look at what was trying to warn you in the past. I'll spare the details because that can be a mini book in itself. Let's just say I found out only my name was listed on the loan as financially liable for the house while both of our names were listed on the deed. It took me some years to surrender over those hard feelings to God and seek and extend forgiveness. Not going to lie to y'all, it was hard. But at the end of it all, things turned out in everyone's favor. Now back to my three months stay in that house.

Since I hadn't yet moved out, I heard day in and day out from my husband about what he was going to do. On one particular day, both of our emotions were at an all-time high. He started yelling and cursing at me and I started yelling and cursing at him. Our daughter walked into the room just as he picked up a metal picture frame and threw it at my head. He then walked over towards me, opened the dresser drawer and slammed it on my fingers. I grabbed my Gerber knife and chased him out of the house. My daughter cried and screamed as loud as she could for us to stop. But we didn't hear her at all because we were bent on vindication.

#coffeemoments Give your children the opportunity to develop their own relationship with their father.

I came to my senses and yelled for my daughter to get into the car and he came and stood between the door and the car. He continued yelling and cursing at me. Instead of trying to push him out, I started attempting to squeeze him in between. He forced his way out and said that he was going to take our daughter from me. I drove off and called my homegirl to see if my daughter and I could stay with her until I found us an apartment. She agreed. The next day, I conducted my day as if nothing had happened the day before, with swollen fingers and everything.

I finally found an apartment for my daughter and me. After some back and forth, the divorce was finalized. I had never lived on my own as an adult before so it was very awkward at first. But I quickly got the hang of things and I loved my newfound freedom.

The courts had granted my daughter's father weekend visits, which turned out to be very hard on her. Seeing us together was all she knew her entire life. Now she was forced to accept the narrative that had been imposed on her without her knowledge or consent. To her, our marriage looked fine. The constant arguing became normal for her. She never expected it to lead to divorce. But ladies, isn't facades what many of us are good at? Not only had the reality of the divorce become her new normal, going to her parents' houses separately, but she was interrogated every time she went to her dad's house. He wanted to know if any other men came around her or came to my house. When I found out, I nipped that in the bud quick.

> **#coffeemoments**
> We can give a good impression and project an image that's so far from the truth until the truth demands to make itself known.

It was difficult, at first, communicating with my ex-husband about anything. He was still stuck on trying to make my life hell. I explained to him that while he did that, he was only hurting our daughter in the long run. He always felt like I bad-mouthed him to her. I reassured him that I didn't have time to sit around and talk about him in any capacity; that she would see for herself what type of man he was. One thing I promised myself a long time ago, was that I would never deny my child's father his right to his child.

Let me pause right here very quick. Ladies, if you're reading this and you're in a position of baby daddy drama, please hear me out. While I understand there are situations where the father isn't permitted to see the child or circumstances are beyond your control, most of the time that's not the case. It's us who keep our children away from the father because of x, y, and z reasons. You only hurt your children more. Don't deny your children their right to see their father just because things didn't work out between you and him. Pause lifted.

> **#coffeemoments**
> Give your children the opportunity to develop their own relationship with their father.

I put a halt to my ex-husband questioning our daughter about anything that went on in my home. I explained he needed to speak directly to me about any questions or concerns he had pertaining to our child. Eventually, we came to an agreement that matters of the house wouldn't be discussed unless it involved our daughter.

Since I was legitimately free and not tied down to anyone, I had my fun. On the weekends my daughter went to her father's house, I got to do some of the things I wanted to without the expectation of entertaining someone else. Sometimes I vegged out on my sofa in front of my television in my sweats (yes, I am a huge sweat pants girl), watching Snapped episodes or my girls called and we'd plan a girls' night out. I started pampering myself as I had always imagined. Treating myself to a nice wine and dinner for one was one of the ways I indulged myself. Another way I indulged myself was to play around with a guy until I got bored. There was this one guy I got caught up on a little bit too long. I started to develop a "more than friends" type mindset towards him but he made it clear to me what he wanted. He was into partying, sex, and alcohol. And while at first, I was into all those things too, I started to feel a void. Like something was missing and that my body was worth more than being used up for another man's pleasure. The icing on the cake for me was when he and I went over to one of his friend's houses.

He walked way ahead of me as I struggled to keep up with him while shuffling in my heels. Now, he had done this a few times before and I tolerated it, but it was something about this time that made me really feel some type of way. I called out to him and told him I was not his dog and that he needed to treat me with a bit more respect. But again, he had already let me know what he wanted out of me. So, how could I put a demand on respect when I was allowing him to dog walk me? Let that marinate sisters because I'm sure you've either been there or are there now. Just know this, it's not worth it.

#coffeemoments
Learn who you are and then you can legitimately put a demand on your value.

When we got to his friend's house, there was another woman there, I assumed it was the guy's girlfriend but then I wasn't sure because of the way he scanned me up and down. My date asked if I could get him a drink. As I got up, I heard a string of expletives trail behind me. I literally heard them talking about every part of my body they could see. I was his arm and bed piece, that was it. Nothing more. That situation-ship ended not long after that.

There were other guys whom I entertained. I felt a deficit. I felt lost. I had carried this feeling with me throughout my entire adult life. I muted it with sex, alcohol, and masks. Just going on and pretending as if everything was fine when it never was. I covered up my internal agony by getting married to a man I never should have married and that ended in divorce. Thoughts of me not being worth nothing flooded my head. I started sleeping with guys again just to shut those voices up. The only thing I was careful about was to not let my daughter see any of this going on. But remember how I said earlier when we as parents aren't careful about the doors we open? That hit me bad and I shut down every situation-ship, bedroom-ship, friends with benefits-ship, all the ships. I had to find some way to declutter my life somehow and especially protect my child from future harm. So, I rode solo. Just her and I. Until I noticed someone else.

Why? As if things couldn't get even more complicated, I noticed him. My daughter and I had gotten used to it being just the two of us and we developed a routine. She became my little homie and I was so cool with that. So, it wasn't like I was trying to look for somebody else.

At first, I just thought the dude was very good looking. Okay, okay, he was fine (lots of emphasis on fine). He worked up at my daughter's child care facility. Even though he caught my eye, I didn't let him know that, at first anyway. However, I showed up was how I showed up. Some days, I would just be coming from the shooting range so I'd be in a dusty uniform, hair all over the place from wearing my Kevlar all day. Other days, I had a chance to slip on some civilian clothes, you know, a little slayage. Something to entertain the eye.

When I noticed I had gotten his attention, he made sure to be at the front desk every time I came in. Our conversation never went beyond "Hey, how are you? Okay well you have a good day." My daughter was in love with him. "Mr. Romon this, Mr. Romon that" I heard it almost every day I picked her up from daycare. Ah, so his name was Romon, got it. So, I figured I'd ask her a few questions about "Mr. Romon." My questions were few and very discreet since my baby was very intelligent for the tender age of 9. I asked if he worked there all the time, if he had children, and was he married. One day, she must have put two and two together because she said, "Hey do you like Mr. Romon?" as she peered at me through my rearview mirror with a mean frown on her face. I responded with I only thought he was handsome and wanted to know more about him. At first, that answer was suffice. But not for too long.

My homegirls and I went out frequently on the weekends. One night, we stepped out to one of the local clubs around town and I saw him. He looked to be by himself, drink in hand, making his rounds around the club. My girls and I decided to post up at one of the tables near the entrance so we could capture the whole club. I hadn't yet told them about him but I kept my eye on him.

The song by Keri Hilson came on, "Pretty Girl Rock." Since this wasn't a break your back type of song, we all played it real cool and swayed and rocked. Drink in my hand, I made sure to catch his eye. I had on a black, white, and pink mini midi skirt, black sheer top, and black strap up stilettos. I was bound to grab his attention so he'd come talk to me. But even though I saw him looking and circling, he never approached me that night.

We played games like this for a while until that magical night at the club, again. This time, I decided that I would show my girls the guy I was digging. When I saw him walk in I pointed him out. Of course, there *has* to be that one girlfriend who makes it so obvious you're talking about somebody. Standing on the dancefloor, she squinted, placed her hands over her eyes shielding them from the light, and said, "Girl I don't see him. Oh, is that him?" as she rapidly pointed in his direction. Epic fail y'all. I slapped her hand down hoping he didn't see the crazy woman pointing at him. I later found out, he did. To kill off the embarrassment, we moved more onto the dancefloor and started dancing with each other.

As if my friends saw a ghost, they both started pointing behind me, grinning from ear to ear. At first, I didn't notice them because I was into the song "No Hands" by Waka Flocka Flame. Remember I'm from Florida, so if you know how we dance down there then you already know.

When I finally looked at them and turned around, I stopped all movement and froze. Mr. *Fine* was right behind me dancing with another girl. A veteran of the dancefloor, I suddenly didn't know what to do. One of my girlfriends came around, grabbed my hand and pulled me even deeper into the crowd on the floor. They had pulled me right next to him. The song had just ended and another one started. Just as I turned around getting ready to head in another direction, I felt a hand touch my waist. I froze again. My girls were squealing like high schoolers as I just stood there. It was Mr. Fine's hand. Without saying anything to each other we just started dancing.

When the song ended, I motioned to step away and he pulled me back up to him. Since he was as good looking as he was, I just knew there was a line of vipers waiting to attack. But he said he didn't want to dance with anybody else and he had his partner for the night, me. Y'all my heart fluttered all over my chest. We danced together for the rest of the night, slow dancing in the middle of the dancefloor, to both slow and fast songs. It was like nobody else was on that dancefloor but the two of us. We held each other close, trying to talk, more like yell in each other's ear.

The last call for alcohol came over the speakers and the lights came on. We all made our way out to the parking lot. My feet were murdering me with each step since I had stood on them the entire night. But I was not going to show an ounce of pain. I stomped in those 5 ½ inch heels like I owned the road. My homegirls decided they wanted to go to Waffle House for a bite to eat. They managed to run some game on two guys who volunteered to pay for their meals.

I went to grab my car door when Romon beat me to it and opened it up for me. A little taken aback, I slowly lowered myself into my seat. He asked for my foot, took my shoe off, and began rubbing my foot, in the parking lot, of the club. I was stunned. This had to be to get some bonus points into letting him come home with me. I asked a slick question, "Oh, so is this what you do to all of your potentials?" He shrugged his shoulders and said, "Nope. You said your feet hurt. So, I decided to rub them. They're not crusty so I rubbed them." Girls, when I tell you my night was all blown away, it most definitely was. I have never in my life had a dude rub my foot at our first encounter.

While he rubbed my foot, I watched with caution. As I mentioned earlier, I had not long ago ended a "situation-ship" with a guy who wanted nothing more than my body and for me to be his arm piece to show off to his homeboys. And like I said, while it was fun in the beginning, I began to get frustrated. I wanted more than just a good time. When I brought that to his attention, he blew me off and said he was only looking for a good time. Got it. Couldn't get mad at him. He made it clear what he wanted and I was clearly entertaining the wrong person. So, I was very cautious from that point on.

My phone rang as I watched Romon slide my shoe back onto my foot. It was one of my homegirls telling me which Waffle House they were heading to. Once he finished, he stood up, gave me a hug, and said he hoped to see me later. We exchanged numbers before he left my car. I sat there for a second reflecting on what had just happened. My phone chirped again and it was Romon. He said he had forgotten to ask which Waffle House we were going to. I told him and he said he'd be right there.

There was something about partying really good and working up a good appetite. Thank goodness for Waffle Houses and IHOP's. When I arrived at the spot, my homegirls were already there with the guys they met earlier. I looked around the small venue and didn't see Romon. So, I squeezed in with them and placed my order. About ten minutes later, his car pulled up in front of the restaurant. My heart started pounding as I moved to another table since there wasn't enough room at the one I was at.

As I sat waiting for Romon to come in, all kinds of thoughts went through my mind. He was a very attractive man and my modus operandi (M.O.) was to skip the small talk and head straight to the bed. But after my last rendezvous with a guy and the icky feeling I got with that and the fact that there was something about Romon that I couldn't shake, I just couldn't go back into freak mode. There was something different I couldn't put my finger on. He wasn't like any other man I had encountered before.

He came in and his amazing scent followed. As we engaged in conversation, I started hoping so badly that he **_wouldn't_** try to make a move or ask to go home with me. We discussed everything from deployments to reading. He was a veteran of the Army. He threw out some authors' names and I was sure he was still trying to run some game on me. Then he threw out some names I hadn't heard of before and showed me a picture of his book collection. He had won me, right then and there. He had stimulated my mind. Of course, I didn't tell him that, but he certainly won.

Late night turned into early morning. I didn't realize we sat in that same spot for 4 hours, talking and laughing! The waitress kept looking over at us, smiling. We finally got up and left, leaving a hefty tip for that waitress. We walked to my car and the whole time I was praying loud and hard in my head. I hadn't gone to church in seemed like forever, but I really needed for God to hear me in that moment. I prayed over and over, "please, God don't let him ask to come home with me. Please, don't let him ask to come home with me. He's different, God, please." Romon leaned over and pecked me on the cheek and told me to make sure I text him when I made it home safely. I smiled so big, y'all and said a shy, girly "oh-kay!"

16

Masterpiece

"Every single one of us are masterpieces, created by
the nail-scarred hands of God."
---Lucrecia Slater

Just as the disciples returned from getting some food, Jesus had just revealed to the Samaritan woman who He was. I can only imagine the looks on the disciples' faces as they watched the woman leave the well. What they saw going on on the outside, a Jewish man talking to a Samaritan woman, paled in comparison to the divine exchange that had just taken place. Jesus deposited a seed into the woman's life that wouldn't only transform her life, but the lives of generations to follow, including today. The most beautiful part about this entire passage is that Jesus never pointed out her flaws. He never ridiculed her for her past. He never shamed her. He knew who she was and what her life was like before ever encountering her. He knew that what He had to offer would create a masterpiece out of her life and affect the lives of everybody she encountered. With her testimony and His blood that Jesus would later shed, created the perfect equation for salvation that continues today and forevermore.

The first few weeks of our budding relationship consisted mostly of us talking daily on the phone with each other. I learned he was a huge fitness/health buff. Well, it's not like I couldn't see that from his physique. We went out to eat around town, just to get to know each other. The more I talked to him the more intrigued I became. He was smooth yet awkward. Funny yet corny. Handsome yet scruffy. And though I know he wasn't, he seemed too perfect for me. But leave it to my daughter, he wasn't good enough.

I hadn't long ago told my daughter about Romon. It was one thing to love "Mr. Romon" at daycare, but to know he was dating her mom was another thing. My daughter was not having it, y'all and she made that very clear. One day, I decided to stop by Romon's apartment for a little bit. I figured since my daughter and Romon had a great relationship at his facility, that things would be fine. Oh, how wrong I was.

As we entered the apartment complex, my daughter said, "Hey, that's Mr. Romon's car! I didn't know he lived over here!" I had that nervous chuckle going on as I replied, "Yeah baby, he does live over here." We pulled up to a parking spot and got out and walked towards his apartment. She asked if I knew anybody over there and whose house were we going to. I told her we were going to see Mr. Romon. She stopped in her tracks. "Why?" was her response, as cold as it could be from a nine-year-old. I stopped with her and said, "Because I want to say hi to him." She riddled me with twenty-one questions and finally said she no longer wanted to go in. After a few minutes, she ended up changing her mind and went inside.

Romon was happy to see us but my daughter made it clear she wasn't happy to see him. It was so awkward. She did her best to make herself loosen up but nothing worked. Romon tried talking to her and nothing. So, our stay wasn't too long.

On the way home after a long silence, my daughter softly asked from the backseat, "Mom, why are you talking to Mr. Romon? Do you love him? You don't love my daddy anymore?" I've seen this kind of stuff take place on television, but I've never witnessed it firsthand. I had experience with divorces related to my mom, but they were very violent and dysfunctional. There was no one to sit me down and explain some of the ins, outs, and realities of divorces. I didn't know what to say. So, I thought back to my childhood and pictured what I would've liked my mother to have told me when we experienced traumatic situations like that. "Baby, I don't love Romon because I don't know him like that. But I do like him and he likes me. Your dad and I aren't together anymore because we couldn't get along. He didn't make me happy anymore and I didn't make him happy anymore. But we both love you! There was nothing you did wrong to cause any of this. Do you understand that?" I looked at her through my rearview mirror and saw her thinking hard about what I said. Then she said, "mom, I can make you happy. You don't need another man to do that. I can." Then she looked back out of the window.

I want to express something very important right here. First, my daughter was absolutely correct in saying that I didn't need another man to make me happy. I think we as women get so caught up in the illusion of a man or a relationship that we lose track of our own presence and source of happiness. Though I hadn't yet fully tapped into that understanding yet, I knew that a man couldn't be the source of my happiness. And second, so often when couples go through breakups or divorces, the children get left wondering what happened and if they were the cause of it. There's little to no explanation to the children because the adults are so busy trying to get back at the other person or pick up the pieces of their lives. Please understand, that though children may not get the full inside scoop on every detail regarding the split.

#coffeemoments
It is so necessary to include them in on this new journey. We aren't the only ones effected by this life change, they are too.

Reassure your children and let them know that though you and the other parent/significant other are no longer together, that you two love the child very much. This may not alleviate all emotional trauma, but at least in the long run, the children will know they weren't left behind and out.

Over the course of the next months, it was rough. Romon continued to stay at his apartment and I stayed at mine. When we all went out together, my daughter gave us a hard time. Thankfully, Romon has years of experience in the children's department. At the time, he didn't have other children (totally blown away y'all, NO KIDS), but he has a degree in childhood education and has worked in that field for several years. So, he knew how to handle difficult situations. Me on the other hand, I'm not going to lie it became frustrating. I blew my head a couple of times on my daughter as I felt she was being too much. Several times, I had to reel my emotions back in and understand where she was coming from.

Things were slowly starting to smooth themselves out but there was still an elephant in the room that Romon and I had to address before we moved forward anymore. He was still married. The last thing I wanted was to inject myself into someone else's relationship, again.

We had been together a few of months and he did tell me in the beginning that he was going through a divorce. I just could no longer shake the thoughts of me getting more attached to him and falling for him and him dropping a bomb on me that he wanted to try and make things work with her. That's never happened to me before, but I've seen it. We had to talk about this. I didn't care how fine he was anymore. I needed answers. If his answers didn't line up with what I had in mind, I was willing to leave him be. Yep, sure was. Because you see, I had already had my bad shares of committing adultery. I hadn't yet discovered what my worth was, but I knew it wasn't in someone else's relationship. And I had made up my mind that the next guy I was going to interact with on any capacity, he and I both would be single, no strings attached anywhere. And I was already risking it. So, Romon had some explaining to do.

Living in his own place didn't mean much to me. My adult years were spent growing up in a military culture. I learned quickly how some guys would come up with deceptive stories just to get what they wanted. I heard all the stories and excuses as to why men were "leaving their wives." Romon explained what happened and that he was indeed in the process of filing for the divorce. But things still didn't sit right with me so I decided to leave him alone anyway.

I told him I would rather be totally out of the picture while he went through the divorce. Should he and his wife decide they wanted to reconcile, the last thing I wanted was to be in the way of that and somehow influence the situation. It was a risk I was willing to take y'all. I liked Romon a lot, but I just could no longer see myself as third fiddle to someone else's relationship. I no longer wanted to be the side chick, side piece, or any other kind of side. So, I broke up with him.

Two months went by since I had heard from Romon. I admit, I was a bit in my feelings because again, I liked him a lot. I had thoughts that maybe they decided to get back together. But I rationalized in my mind that if that was the case, there was not much for me to lose out on since we hadn't been together that long. He and I hadn't been physical beyond a hug and the kiss he gave me on the cheek. I felt a little pride for that fact. He was the first guy I hadn't jumped all over after barely or not knowing him at all. As I thought about that, my phone rang. It was Romon.

"Hey, what's up? What are you doing?" he asked. I was so stinking excited to hear that deep, baritone voice on the other end of my phone.

But of course, I had to play it cool. "Not much, just laying on the sofa watching Snapped" I said. Fort Campbell and other military installations had what was called DONSA's or Day of No Scheduled Activities, so all military personnel were off that day. And I was doing one of my favorite past times, on my sofa, in my sweats, watching a Snapped marathon. I asked how he was doing and what he was up to. He said he was just getting ready to head out on his lunch break. I wanted so badly to ask about his personal affairs, but I restrained myself. But I remember I told him not to contact me until he had taken care of whatever business he needed to take care of. And that was regardless of what his decision was. So, I assumed (not much) that things had been taken care of because we were sitting on the phone with each other.

We had some small talk, then he said, "So, remember I said I don't like watching scary movies? Well, the only way I'd watch one was if I was with you." Oh-kay. Crickets. I chuckled a bit because his corny-ness was truly coming through. "Okay, I got that. But what are you trying to say? Wait, are you trying to ask me out to a movie?" It came to me mid-sentence that that's exactly what he was trying to do. "Yes, I am actually. Maybe I should start over. Yeah, let me start over. Lucrecia, would you like to go to the movies with me?" I blushed so hard my cheeks and ears felt like they had just caught on fire. But he wasn't out of the pits yet. "It all depends," I said. I didn't realize how tensed my body was until I caught a cramp in my thigh. He knew exactly what I was referring to and responded with, "You're good. All is taken care of. Now will you go to the movies with me?" "I'd love to," I said with a huge smile on my face.

We went to Nashville to explore a bit downtown. I decided not to dress up since we were doing a lot of walking. But I got the feeling no matter how I dressed, I was pleasing to Romon's eye. From that day on, we were literally inseparable. We shopped together, clubbed together, everything. Soon, I was picking up some of his past time habits, such as watching hours of CNN. I'm cracking up as I write this because that man has not changed one bit.

After I knew Romon and I were going to officially call ourselves a couple, I told my daughter. Although she knew we liked each other, she didn't know details. Of course, I didn't let her in to every waking detail of our relationship, but I believe her seeing that I truly cared for her feelings, impacted her. Slowly, she started loosening up around him a little bit more. Things remained incredibly awkward for her at daycare though as her friends started to learn of our relationship. But she became friendly again with Romon again. She started talking to him and playing around with him more. This was my princess's new narrative. One she didn't ask for but would have to live through.

h

Romon and I had an incredible relationship. But I knew I was still very guarded. I shared with him what I wanted him to know. I wanted to share everything with him, but how could I? How would I look in his eyes? There was one thing that made its way out without me even saying anything. Secrets have ways y'all.

#coffeemoments
They have tricks up their sleeves and if we're not careful to take care of and get rid of them, they will make themselves known on their own.

My man was a very carefree, peace, and harmony type of dude. He disliked drama and any type of confusion. He loved to please me with gifts and just do things to make me happy. I was appreciative, but remember those demons I mentioned earlier, yeah, those jokers started making their appearance right back into my life.

There almost wasn't a day that went by where I wasn't yelling at my daughter or going off on Romon for something. Neither of them knew which part of me they were getting. Romon and I hadn't yet moved in together, but he came over for dinner. I would literally be fine the first minute and the next, I'm snapping on him or my daughter.

One night, it got so bad that Romon just up and left. I was so hot in my feelings that I didn't care. The next day, he called and dropped a truth bomb right on my heart. He said, "I've been thinking to myself, can I live with this for the next ten to fifteen years of my life? Do I want to live with this? I'm not a drama type of guy and your attitude is terrible! What did I ever do to you?" In defense, I started bringing up my ex-husband and rambling on and on about him. Romon said in his defense, "I'm not him. Don't penalize me for what he couldn't or didn't do." He ended the conversation and that was it. Just. Like. That. Talk about a huge slap in my face, on both cheeks!

Ladies, how often do we do that? Gone ahead and tell the truth. We place unrealistic expectations on the next man because we were left hurt. Instead of us taking the time to soul-search, we hop into another relationship expecting it to be something we've conjured up in our heads. And then when the guy falls short, we lash out. This is what I've learned and this is what I want you to take away. As long as you place yourself in the position to be used, you will continue to get used. As long as you refuse to confront and address those inner demons, you will always be tormented. No relationship, no amount of sex, drugs, alcohol, shopping, or fakery will ever be able to cover that up.

> **#coffeemoments**
> You must learn to own your hurt. Own your dysfunction. Own your truth and dare yourself to do something about it.

I didn't hear from Romon for the next few of days. Instead of me taking heed to what he said, I became angrier. I didn't realize how bad things were until I verbally hurt my daughter. This was where the rubber hit the road. She came to me one afternoon with a face full of tears. Her words I will never forget, "Mom, why do you have to yell at me all the time instead of talking to me? Just talk to me!" She turned and walked back to her room, leaving me dumbfounded at the dining room table. Hot tears streamed down my face because I knew something was wrong, I just couldn't put my finger on it.

I tried my hand at counseling once right after I returned from Iraq, but told those counselors to kick rocks for trying to medicate me without even trying to take the time to understand my why. But doing nothing was getting me nowhere and creating innocent victims so I tried again. I self-enrolled into a mental help program based off a referral to a new counselor at Adult Behavioral Health on post. When I went to my first appointment, I already had it made up in my mind that if she came out of her mouth sideways about some dog on medication, I was going to walk right out. But she didn't. She didn't at all.

The first appointment was weird. She asked questions to get to know me, but I was very reserved and guarded. I still wasn't too trusting but I sensed this counselor wasn't like the last one. The appointment ended quickly and I hurried out, not to be seen. Though I really didn't say much to the counselor, I kind of looked forward to going back.

We were about three appointments in when I unintentionally spilled all the beans of my life. I can't remember the question, but whatever my counselor asked, was a trigger question. I remember going through half the box of tissues talking about everything from my current situation to when I was three-years-old and what I had witnessed. It was apparent I had carried many "bags" with me through my life.

My counselor proved to be one of the greatest support systems when I learned that a soldier/friend in my unit had been killed in Afghanistan. I've never mourned someone the way I did for him. One of the most loving men I had ever known had received his eternal crown. I was mad at God for taking him. He was such a God-fearing, God-loving, family man. At the time, I named off several people God could've taken in his place. Just being real. To this day, I think of him often and even cry sometimes. But I know he served a purpose and made an impact in my life and the lives of so many others.

Because of my injuries sustained in Iraq from my last deployment, the military decided to conduct a medical board on me. That means, I had to go through extensive testing and exams to see if I was still fit for duty. If not, higher medical command would decide if I would be medically chaptered or retired. The whole process was exhausting. Day after day, I had appointments lined up only for doctors to poke and prod. I looked forward to my times with my counselor since she had become my safe place.

Some sessions resulted in us laughing at something silly, but many sessions involved me cleansing through tears and boxes of tissues, bouts of anger at God for taking my friend, or frustrations with this whole medical board process. She really took a lot from me. But never once did she even give off a hint that she was passing judgment or being insensitive to my needs. I understand it was her job, but it was also more than that. She too, was a human being as I was, and she respected that. Sisters, let me encourage you to get the help if you need it. Stop allowing other people's fears, insecurities, or your own thoughts to prevent you from receiving the help you need. Mental health is huge and it's paramount for our overall health.

#coffeemoments
We can't be anything to anyone if we don't first take care of ourselves.

To lighten the mood during one of my sessions, my counselor told me of a dream she'd had of me. She said she saw herself in the dream holding a baby and the baby was mine. I laughed because even though Romon and I had talked about children, we weren't in a rush Kimarra was just enough for the moment and besides that was like starting over considering my daughter was already eleven years old. Oh, how my counselor had jokes.

Just as I was getting used to being with only my counselor, she made an announcement that she was starting a group for other women and she wanted me to be a part of it. I was extremely apprehensive at first. She became my safe place and I didn't know how I felt about involving other people that deep into my life. Through reassurance, she convinced me to join. It was amazing. I connected with other soldiers from different walks of life, races, and ages. Through our brokenness we developed bonds. My counselor made it clear that the group was a "no judgment" zone. We all respected each other and supported each other. We came together and celebrated when one of us overcame a hurdle. And we also came together to mourn as we lost one of our own group sisters. I didn't learn of her passing until after I returned from my birthday. I was devastated because we had just made plans to connect with each other outside of group. I felt myself shutting down again because of her loss. I got so tired of people coming and going in my life. But I had to make myself realize that that situation was not about me, it was about Joelle. It was about the obstacles she faced and the victories she won before her life ended. I will never forget her.

17

For a Time, Such as This

"And who knows whether you have attained royalty
for such a time as this [and for this very purpose]?"
---Esther 4:14, Amplified Version

*The woman at the well served a very important purpose in history.
Generations were impacted by her life at the well. By now, you all know
that her life had purpose. And I want to encourage you that yours does
too. Yes, sister, every single broken piece of your life serves purpose.
Once the woman at the well was sure who she talked to was the Messiah,
she left everything behind and went to tell the others. Do you see that?
She went BACK to the very people who rejected her and told them of the
Messiah! When our lives have been touched by the hands of God, those
who once saw us as nothing or we saw as enemies, all of that becomes
irrelevant. What becomes important is that we were touched by God and
now we want everyone we meet to experience the same thing. So, I want
to encourage you not to withhold from God because so many are waiting
on your testimony.*

I had been working with my counselor for about a year. We tried several
techniques since I didn't want to be medicated, but trying to keep up
with manual therapy was overwhelming. Don't get me wrong, there were
positive changes. I was making progression, but it wasn't as fast as my
counselor and I would've liked. So, she suggested I just try medication. If
I didn't like it, I could get off. I was hesitant but I decided to give it a try.

Before she put in the prescription, she suggested I take a pregnancy
test. What? For what? I know I'm not pregnant! I thought. Romon and I

did dance around the ideal that if ever had a child, a girl, we would name her Troi, from the movie "Crooklyn" by Spike Lee. We watched that movie several times, mainly because of the cute little boss mama named Troi. The name was different and very unique. But that was only a thought. I laughed but told my counselor, I'd take the test.

That evening I sat in my bathroom stunned. Two very dark pink lines showed up on the test. I was most definitely pregnant, at least according to the test. I'd bought two tests just in case the first was didn't work. I took the second one, same. I promise the lines looked darker on the second test than the first one. I called Romon right away. He had just walked into his apartment when I told him the news. He cursed in excitement and said, "so I'm going to be a dad, huh?"

I was overjoyed but very scared. I was literally starting over. Romon had no children of his own so I didn't know how he was going to be as a parent, although I suspected he'd make an incredible father. Then my excitement fizzled. I had to tell Kimarra. She had well gotten used to Romon, but how was she going to react to new baby news?

I decided to tell her on my way to PT the next morning. I was going to drop her off at daycare and made up my mind that I'd tell her then. And Romon had been transferred to another facility so she wouldn't have to worry about looking in his face all day with this news fresh on her brain. "So, what would you think of being a big sister?" I glanced at her in the rearview mirror. She thought about it then said, "I don't know. Why?" I asked another question, "what if I told you you were going to be a big sister?" Her eyes got as big as half-dollars. "Mom, are you pregnant?" she asked almost yelling. I said yes and chuckled a bit. I could feel the sweat starting to saturate my PT uniform. She asked if I was just playing and when I said no, she became quiet. We arrived at her daycare facility. I hugged her and gave her a kiss on the cheek. Had I made the right decision? I worried about Kimarra. I worried about how she took all of this and where her place was in this growing family. And even though I tried taking things slowly, things certainly weren't trying to slow down.

Once I notified my unit that I was pregnant, things started to get real. I had to get reissued new maternity uniforms. Oh my goodness, the most hideous looking but comfortable uniforms ever. I was placed on a pregnancy profile which, really, didn't change much of what I was already restricted from doing since I was pending being medical boarded.

I realized the apartment I lived in wasn't going to be big enough for the new baby. So, I prepared to move out. Romon decided that he wanted to be with me in this journey, so we decided to move in together.

On top of that, he yearned for his youngest sister to come live with him. So, we arranged for that to happen also. Now, check this out y'all. I won't lie, I thought the little girl in a picture Romon once showed me was his daughter, not his sister. After meeting his mom, she confirmed that the little girl was indeed his sister. She and my daughter have almost the same exact name and are both the same age, three weeks apart with my daughter being the oldest. Talk about divine orchestration.

When my daughter learned that Romon's sister was coming to live with us, she was too excited. Now, she didn't have to worry about being the only kid around the house. She literally had an unconventional twin. Romon's dad and stepmother came up from Atlanta to help us move and settle into our new home. They were over the moon to learn their son was going to be a daddy. I was happy to be so welcomed into the family. Neither of us thought anything about getting married. We were just happy to be creating a family. Looking back, I see exactly how God planned all of this out, for a time such as this.

Romon's sister arrived in the summer of 2012. We threw her a huge welcome party and celebrated her arrival. Things were great in the beginning, but any of you reading this who either have teenagers or have raised teenagers, understand that good can quickly turn to bad.

Romon and I decided to attend church regularly since we wanted to instill a firm spiritual foundation into our kids. But here is something funny. I thought Romon was an atheist, at least a borderline atheist. I mean, he had a slight belief in God but had so many questions. And these questions weren't out of curiosity. They seemed more out of disbelief.

There was this one woman he told me about at his job who always invited him to her church. Consistently, he turned her down. I'm not sure what transpired in his mind, but a little before I got pregnant, he decided we should go. It was New Year's Eve 2011. While I was ready and sure that we were going to pop bottles and turn up at somebody's club, he suggested we go to church instead. While I wasn't against the idea, it had been a while since I last attended because of being hurt by previous church leadership. And I wasn't necessarily in a church going mood and on top of that, I was shocked he even made the suggestion. But we went. And although we weren't committed or anything like that, we attended off and on. I am constantly amazed at how God will use people for His good. That woman, whom her and I are cool with today, was a catalyst to get us exactly where God needed us to be. Thank you if you're reading this.

When we went to church, we never tried faking the funk of being married or anything that we weren't. However, most of the congregation assumed we were married. People may have been fooled on the outside, but God was making it clear that He knew we weren't married. One sermon in particular, confirmed that. The pastor preached a sermon titled "Leaving Lust-Vegas." I don't think I've ever been so uncomfortable in church before in my life. Conviction flooded me everywhere. Every topic discussed hit on our situation. Even though Romon was an amazing man and I knew he'd be a great dad, essentially, I was giving him all the benefits of a wife without the lifelong commitment agreement of marriage from him.

Now, I understand this new age way of thinking, that marriage isn't everything or even relevant or necessary. And while I don't have time or space to get deep into that discussion, just understand this. Marriage was created by God for very specific reasons. One of which, spiritually, it is a sacred display of commitment between Him and His human bride, us. We are to demonstrate through our outward expressions of marriage, a vow to God that will last forever. Practically speaking, the commitment of marriage makes the statement that both the man and woman willingly sacrifice their wants and desires, and will to become one with the other and to live life out with the other person, forever.

I asked Romon on the way home from church that day if he felt uncomfortable with the message preached. He said a cool, "Nope, sure didn't" while I was getting torn up in my heart. I knew we were living in sin because we weren't married, but neither of us was ready to take that step yet. We knew we wanted to eventually get married, just not at that moment. So, we put the thoughts off. And enters baby into the world.

The entire pregnancy we opted not to learn the gender of the baby. I was so tempted to, but since this was Romon's first child, I wanted to honor his wishes so I waited to. October 3, 2012, I gave birth to my hefty bundle of love, Satroyia "Troi" Slater. She was a whopping 9 pounds 10 ounces and 23 inches long. She was perfection. A child who came after all the trash in my life, she was my new beginning. Romon's mom flew in from Florida and his sister who is in the Army, came to witness the miracle of our baby girl's life. I felt so honored for God to give me such a beautiful blessing. Yet, even through all the beauty, God was still nudging us to get ourselves together.

About a month after Troi was born, I sat in the girls' room messing around with them when Romon busted through the door. He started talking crazy talk about price tags on rings and all that stuff. Then he said (as corny but as cute as ever) "Girl, if I give you this ring, you better respect it. If I give you this ring, you're gonna be my girl for life." Wait, what? I felt weak. Was this man proposing to me? The girls started screaming as Romon got down on one knee and asked me to be his wife. I cried so hard y'all. I had never been proposed to and I didn't have to buy the ring. That joker was beautiful too! Of course, I said YES!

A few days after Christmas of 2012, I noticed Romon wasn't doing too well. We assumed it was something he'd eaten. I woke up to him vomiting in the bathroom. Being the investigator I was and having a cast-iron stomach, I got up to take a look. I was shocked by what I saw so I looked up Romon's symptoms. Over the next couple of days, I watched Romon deteriorate. His skin went from a beautiful dark chocolate complexion to a dull grey color. I urged him to let me take him to the hospital because I was scared. But he depended so much on his good health and shape to pull him through.

When he told me his standing heart rate was way faster than it should've been and that he'd passed out a few times, I put an end to all of this. I told him I was taking him regardless of what he said, but he agreed. The girls grabbed the baby, her bag, and their things and rushed into the car. Everyone cried so loudly because we just knew we were about to lose Romon. He wailed and wiggled in pain in the front seat as he kept grabbing his head saying how badly it was hurting. I floored the gas pedal to the floor and pushed my car to the governor. A police officer was going to have to chase me all the way to the hospital because I wasn't stopping. When we arrived, I could smell an odor coming from Romon. It's the odor I became familiar with working with my mom when she started working for a nursing home. It was a death smell. I prayed to myself, "Please God don't let me lose him. Please don't take him." With my help, Romon staggered into the emergency room and he was immediately admitted to the back. I didn't want to leave the girls out in the lobby by themselves with the baby, so I stayed out there with them. But you better believe, I bugged the mess out of the receptionist every fifteen minutes. The girls told me to go ahead and go back and they'd watch the baby.

When I went back, I burst into tears. Romon had all kinds of wires and tubes coming out his body. I asked what happened and what he and the doctors told me shook me to my core. Apparently, Romon had two ulcers in his stomach that ruptured. For days they bled out which is why his vomit and bowls were the color they were. His headaches in the back of his head were caused from rapid drops in his blood pressure. Romon lost a total of four pints of blood and needed a transfusion immediately. The doctors were amazed that they were even talking to him. He should not have survived that. But God says, for a time such as this we've been called.

The next few months, I watched my family transform. Where my husband used to credit his good health and even his survival off of how healthy and strong he was, I watched him surrender it all and himself to God. He didn't even cry when his daughter was born and here I was, watching a full grown 6-foot 200-pound man, fall to his knees crying. My entire family got saved and filled with the Holy Spirit. But of course, you didn't expect us to just ride on clouds and that be it, did you?

Because baby girl was so big during my pregnancy, I developed an umbilical hernia that needed immediate repair. I had to wait at least three months after giving birth because I had a C-section with her. After I had surgery to repair the hernia, trouble almost immediately started. A week after surgery, I was throwing up blood and had already had two visits to the emergency room. The last visit, the doctors decided to keep me for three days. They didn't know what was wrong, but kept me under close observation. I was in the absolute worse pain I've ever experienced. I hate medicine, but because of the pain, I had no choice but to take it. That was the loneliest hospital stay I had ever had.

One of those nights, God spoke to me. He made it clear that He needed me to get myself together because there were things He needed me to do for His kingdom. I was saved, but we were still living in sin by not being married and there were still bags I was holding onto from my past. I had to let them go.

And I want to encourage you too, sis, you must let them go. You, me, we, can't effectively do what God has called us to do if we're still lugging around the baggage. Those bags were never meant for us to carry. When you play cards, you're dealt a hand. But it doesn't mean you keep the cards in your hand. You dish them out. You throw them out. That's the same thing for that baggage. And I started letting them go, but with a cost.

> #coffeemoments
> Sisters, if we keep holding onto dead weight, in whatever manner or package that weight comes in, we will kill ourselves. Sometimes figuratively, sometimes physically. Let the bags go.

Two months after my hospital stay, Romon and I got married. There were no fancy arrangements or décor. The church wasn't packed to the max with guests. Just us, our kids, his sister, his family from Georgia, a handful of church members, and the pastor. It was small, but somehow everything I'd ever wanted. Now that Romon and I had done our part, it was God's turn to do His. It was time for Him to clean some house.

There's a couple of scriptures I'm reminded of that talks about refining. Isaiah 48:10 (NLT) says, *"I have refined you, but not as silver is refined. Rather, I have refined you in the furnace of suffering."* And 1 Peter 1:7 (NLT) *"These trials will show that your faith is genuine. It is being tested as fire tests and purifies gold—though your faith is far more precious than mere gold. So, when your faith remains strong through many trials, it will bring you much praise and glory and honor on the day when Jesus Christ is revealed to the whole world."* Merriam-Webster's Dictionary defines refine as: to free from moral imperfection: ELEVATE. You see, I was willing to surrender all back to God, but I didn't realize the cost. God understands we will never be perfect on this side of heaven. However, He can bring us as close to godliness and holiness in our human forms. And one way He does that is through refinement. I'm not going to say that every bad situation we encounter comes from God because that's just not the truth. However, I do believe God will allow some things to happen to us or use our own frail decisions to teach, prune, mature, and refine us. And that's exactly what happened.

We needed His strength like never before when my family was hit hard with financial trouble and I was hit with another hard round of depression. We went through two years of financial turmoil and I honestly didn't see how we were coming out of it. I fought daily with negative thoughts. And wouldn't God have the nerve to bring up that vision He gave me in 2006! Like, really God? Now? I could barely think straight and here it was God bringing that vision up to me and talking to me in the shower about a ministry He needed me to start up. Y'all I was done. I was overwhelmed.

I sought out counseling at the Veteran's Affairs hospital because I knew depression was trying to take over. And what God was showing me was just too much. How was I supposed to carry all that stuff out when we didn't have two pennies to rub together? How when my mind was so way off? How when I still wrestled with God with giving up my bags? If there's nothing else I've learned about God, it's that He is extremely patient. He understands the ins and outs of the human experience better than we do, that's part of why He gifts us with grace. And a whole lot of grace is what I needed to get through.

Slowly, we came out of the refinement season, for the time being anyway. I started my blog, **Authentically Spoken,** in August 2014. I was scared and worried about how my thoughts would be taken by the public, but I kept writing. My husband and I gleaned from several lessons we learned through the past few years and committed to making better decisions with our money.

Late 2015, God presented us with the gift of building our very first home together! As we walked through the frame of the home, in February of 2016, God spoke to my heart. He said He was giving us this home off the condition that we would use it as not only our home, but a place of ministry. How that looked, we didn't know, but Romon and I came into agreement that we would be obedient. June 2016, we moved into our first home. It too came with a process, but we allowed God to be with us every step of the way.

Walking through the doors of our new home was surreal. Not just physically, but in so many other ways.

Here was this broken, poor, dysfunctional girl turned woman from the ghetto of Florida, who was told she wouldn't be anything and that she was stupid and ugly, now standing on the floor of her own home. She was far from perfect and having it all together. But she made a covenant with God that He owned her life. She made a promise to Him that this time, she wouldn't leave His side and no matter how hard it got, she would fight with everything in her. She went into partnership with her Father to share her story with as many who would read or listen, in hopes that they would be freed from their own personal prisons.

That woman is me. And I encourage you sister to be set free.

Conclusion

Broken, But Beautifully Restored

Sisters, if there was one thing that stood out to you in this book, I hope it was knowing how amazingly crazy in love God is with you and how much He wants to see you win. My life was riddled with many holes. Some have healed and some are still healing. But it's not over and it's not the end. Until my breath leaves my body, it's not over. And I want you to develop the same type of mentality. Of course, it won't be easy. I haven't heard of any type of recovery that was a piece of cake. Emotional wounds occur over time, so time is needed to heal, not saying that time heals all wounds, but time is necessary. Don't delay anymore by continuing to self-sabotage your recovery. We've done that too long and the buck stops here. Even though God presented me with the idea to write this book, I still could've decided not to and I was very close to not writing it or completing it. I was too embarrassed and humiliated to reveal half of this stuff to anybody, let alone the entire world. The only ones who knew my nasty and my crazy were the ones who were just as messed up as I was. It wasn't until I took God for real and started letting Him really enter my life and do work, that I decided to journey forward with writing. The more I wrote, the more I saw my children. The more I saw their future, their legacy being unaffected by the generational trash that followed me for so long. God literally took me through several scriptures as proof of why this book needed to be and why I needed to be as raw as I had to be. One scripture was Proverbs 31:8-9 (NLT) "Speak up for those who cannot speak for themselves; ensure justice for those being crushed. Yes, speak up for the poor and helpless, and see that they get justice." There are women who wouldn't dare share some of the dark details of their lives. For various reasons, but one, I'm sure is out of fear. Fear has been the number one killer of dreams and freedom for many of us. We've allowed fear to hold us prisoner and rule over every decision of our lives. I'm not going to call myself a hero, superwoman, super feminist, or any of that. But I knew the importance of me sharing my story was vital to God. Some women will only see God through my words. Another scripture was Revelation 12:11(AMP) "And they overcame and conquered him because of the blood of the Lamb and because the word of their testimony..." I learned the value in these words: **sharing, vulnerability, transparency, me too, and testimony.** Each word serves as weapons in being set free and healed from sin and emotional trauma. I was a part of a women's group at a church I attended and in that group, was the first time I admitted some of my sins to other church goers. It was people of the church I was most afraid of being judged and ridiculed. But in that moment, I knew God was nudging me to share. And I did. Over the course of time, I was healed and restored. Sisters, let me explain something to you. People will always have an opinion or criticism. There will always be someone lurking and seeking to make your life worse than what it already is. When God presents a door for you to run through, take it. Don't get so caught up in what people will say. When you can get engrained in your mind that people, yes even church people, are just as tattered and torn as you, making those steps towards restoration becomes a bit more tolerable. I often sit on my back deck and just stare at the woods. I love the scenery because it takes my mind off the noise. I'm reminded of the personal inbox messages I receive on my social media accounts or text messages or face to face conversations. And my eyes fill with tears. I know I'm not worthy of this calling. But I am forever grateful and humble that God chose me. My immediate family still resides in Florida. I don't get the opportunity to speak with them often because there's still so much hurt, strife, and painful areas that need healing, but I know God isn't done with them either. Just as He has and is working on me, so is He with them. And I'll say this as encouragement to you. Just because you're smack in the middle of God's will, doesn't mean everything will magically realign and become perfect. There will still be broken relationships to address, bad habits to kick, and maturity to develop. Life will continue to throw its best and worst. You must decide that you will daily submit to God's will anyway, commit to do what you can, and submit the rest to Him. So, I want to leave you with this question sis, what if I told you that purpose rests in every broken, checkered piece of your life, would you believe me?

Lucrecia

References

National Coalition Against Domestic Violence. (2010). National Statistics. Retrieved from http://ncadv.org/learn-more/statistics

Pretend. (n.d.). In Merriam-Webster's dictionary. Retrieved from https://www.merriam webster.com/dictionary/pretend

Refine. (n.d.). In Merriam-Webster's dictionary. Retrieved from https://www.merriam webster.com/dictionary/refine

Domestic Violence Hotline Contact Information1-800-799-7233 (SAFE) or 1-800-787-3224 (TTY)

For the blog post "The Bags Gotta Go" that was mentioned in the book, I invite you to either click here or copy & paste this link into your browser to read the full blog. http://lsslater.com/index.php/2017/04/05/the-bags-gotta-go/

Made in the USA
Monee, IL
04 August 2020

37592301R00094